At Issue

The Right to Die

Other Books in the At Issue Series:

At Issue

The Right to Die

Tamara Thompson, Book Editor

GREENHAVEN PRESS
A part of Gale, Cengage Learning

GALE
CENGAGE Learning·

Farmington Hills, Mich • San Francisco • New York • Waterville, Maine
Meriden, Conn • Mason, Ohio • Chicago

Elizabeth Des Chenes, *Director, Content Strategy*
Douglas Dentino, *Manager, New Product*

For more information, contact:
Greenhaven Press
27500 Drake Rd.
Farmington Hills, MI 48331-3535
Or you can visit our Internet site at www.gale.cengage.com

For product information and technology assistance, contact us at

Gale Customer Support, 1-800-877-4253

For permission to use material from this text or product, submit all requests online at www.cengage.com/permissions.

Further permissions questions can be e-mailed to permissionrequest@cengage.com.

Articles in Greenhaven Press anthologies are often edited for length to meet page requirements. In addition, original titles of these works are changed to clearly present the main thesis and to explicitly indicate the author's opinion. Every effort is made to ensure that Greenhaven Press accurately reflects the original intent of the authors. Every effort has been made to trace the owners of copyrighted material.

Cover photograph copyright © Images.com/Corbis.

LIBRARY OF CONGRESS CATALOGING-IN-PUBLICATION DATA

Right to die (Tamara Thompson) The right to die / Tamara Thompson, book editor.
  pages cm. -- (At issue)
  Summary: "The At Issue series includes a wide range of opinion on a single controversial subject. Each volume includes primary and secondary sources from a variety of perspectives -- eyewitnesses, scientific journals, government officials and many others. Extensive bibliographies and annotated lists of relevant organizations to contact offer a gateway to future research"-- Provided by publisher.
  Summary: "At Issue: The Right to Die: Books in this anthology series focus a wide range of viewpoints onto a single controversial issue, providing in-depth discussions by leading advocates, a quick grounding in the issues, and a challenge to critical thinking skills"-- Provided by publisher.
  Includes bibliographical references and index.
  ISBN 978-0-7377-6850-3 (hardback) -- ISBN 978-0-7377-6851-0 (paperback)
  1. Right to die--Juvenile literature. 2. Assisted suicide--Juvenile literature. 3. Medical ethics--Juvenile literature. I. Thompson, Tamara, editor. II. Title.
  R726.R4975 2014
  179.7--dc23
                                                                    2013044031

Printed in the United States of America
  2 3 4 5 6   18 17 16 15 14

Contents

Introduction

In 2009, a gracious and articulate woman named Cody Curtis allowed filmmakers to follow her deeply personal journey with terminal liver cancer and to document her decision to end her life using Oregon's Death with Dignity Act. One of only three states to do so, Oregon's law makes it legal for physicians to provide "aid-in-dying" for terminally ill but mentally competent adults who have just a few months left to live. As she wasted away from the cruel disease, Curtis asked her doctor for a prescription for life-ending medication. Then she spent several months enjoying quality time and creating memories with her loved ones. When the pain and suffering from the cancer became simply unbearable, she invited friends and family to her bedside to say goodbye as she took the medication that peacefully ended her life. She was fifty-four years old.

But although Curtis's manner of death was publicly celebrated and entirely legal in the state of Oregon, it would not have been in most other places in the country.

In February 2013, Philadelphia nurse Barbara Mancini handed her terminally ill ninety-three-year-old father a vial of the narcotic painkiller morphine. He took it from her and drank it, and he soon slipped into unconsciousness. When discovered by a hospice worker a short time later, he was rushed to the hospital and revived, against the wishes specified in his end-of-life medical care directive. He died four days later, and his daughter now faces murder charges under a statute that makes it illegal to assist a suicide. (Mancini maintains she was simlpy trying to ease her father's pain, not help him end his life—something the US Supreme Court has ruled is legal, even if it hastens death.)

The vastly different ways that these two states handle the legalities of end-of-life decision-making is reflective of the current national landscape on the issue. Only three states have laws that explicitly allow people to end their own lives under limited conditions—Oregon (1994), Washington (2008), and Vermont (2013). Montana permits it under a 2009 state court decision that rules physicians cannot be prosecuted for prescribing life-ending medications. Thirty-four states currently prohibit assisted suicide outright, and seven others ban it through legal precedent. Euthanasia, in which a doctor or other third party actively administers a lethal medication to a patient—rather than the patient administering it to themselves—is illegal in every state.

With aging baby boomers (the seventy-seven million people born between 1946 and 1964) reaching their senior years and beginning to face end-of-life decisions themselves, however, public opinion is starting to shift on the right-to-die question. When Massachusetts voters narrowly rejected a law based on the Oregon statute in 2012 (49 percent yes to 51 percent no), it raised public awareness and sparked a national dialogue on the issue. As a result, a push to legalize physician-assisted suicide is now underway in half a dozen states.

According to the National Conference of State Legislatures, a bipartisan nongovernmental organization that tracks legislative trends, bills legalizing physician-assisted dying are now being considered in Connecticut, New Jersey, Kansas, and Hawaii, as well as a second attempt in Massachusetts. There are also end-of-life, choice-related bills under consideration in New Hampshire, New York, Arizona, and Montana, the group reports.

While proponents of such laws argue that they preserve the dignity and personal autonomy of dying individuals and are a compassionate alternative to suffering intractable pain or unwanted medical interventions, critics say they are little more than euphemistic legal cover for putting someone to death. Such laws are not about the right to die, they argue, but rather the right to kill.

"Assisted suicide seems, at first blush, like a good thing to have available," the Disability Rights Education and Defense Fund (DREDF) asserts on its website. "But on closer inspection, there are many reasons legalization is a very serious mistake. Supporters often focus solely on superficial issues of choice and self-determination. It is crucial to look deeper."

For a broad range of groups that oppose so-called Death with Dignity laws—from advocates for vulnerable populations like the disabled, mentally ill, poor or elderly, to religious groups who oppose it for spiritual reasons—looking deeper means recognizing that no matter how well a law is written, it can have dire unintended consequences. Among the concerns frequently cited:

- People who are experiencing depression may be granted help to end their lives instead of getting effective mental health treatment.

- The terminally ill may act on real or perceived pressure from caregivers to hurry up and get their deaths over with so they are no longer a burden.

- The elderly may choose aid-in-dying because they feel financial pressure from relatives due to the high cost of late-life care and the knowledge that dying sooner means more money left for inheritances.

- The ability of a doctor to prescribe lethal drugs can undermine the doctor-patient relationship and erode trust in the health-care system.

- The disabled may experience discrimination from able-bodied people that leads them to erroneously devalue their abilities and the worth of their own lives.

- Individuals who are told they have terminal illnesses and only months to live sometimes defy the odds and live much longer or recover altogether.

A more general and widespread concern, however, is that allowing any form of physician-assisted dying could prove to be a deadly combination with the nation's profit-driven health-care system. The concern is that physicians would have an incentive to cut costs by dispensing lethal medications that are a fraction of the cost of life-saving or life-extending treatments, or that insurance companies and HMOs would agree to cover the cost of helping someone die, but not helping them live.

"The deadly impact of legalizing assisted suicide would fall hardest on socially and economically disadvantaged people who have less access to medical resources and who already find themselves discriminated against by the health care system," writes the DREDF.

The authors in *At Issue: The Right to Die* discuss key issues involved in the end-of-life debate and explore the legality and morality of Death with Dignity laws, aid-in-dying, physician-assisted death, assisted suicide, euthanasia, and the right-to-die movement.

1

A History of the Right to Die

National Center for Life and Liberty

The National Center for Life and Liberty is a Christian-focused nonprofit legal ministry that works to defend life and liberty freedoms nationwide. The organization's president and general counsel, David Gibbs III, was the lead attorney in the landmark Terri Schiavo case, representing Schiavo's parents as they fought efforts to disconnect their daughter's feeding tube.

The concept that people are entitled to the right to die took a long time to develop in the United States, and popular and legal acceptance of the idea was based on several high-profile cases. Over four decades, the cases of Karen Ann Quinlan, Nancy Cruzan, Estelle Browning, and Terri Schiavo each set new legal precedents concerning the right to die. Each case furthered the right of individuals or their caregivers to discontinue life support, stop medical treatment, or withhold food and water. These cases also brought about the common use of living wills and advance directives, legal documents that allow people to clearly state their end-of-life care wishes while they are still healthy and able to do so.

Most Americans are able to identify *Roe v. Wade* as the 1973 United States Supreme Court case that established a constitutional right for women to abort their unborn babies at the beginning of life. However, not many Americans are able to similarly identify the important court cases that paved the way for "right to die" laws and the acceptance of euthanasia or mercy killing in America. This new constitutional so-called "right to die" involves the ability to terminate those at the end of life—many of whom are elderly or disabled, or who lack a particular "quality of life" or whose care is determined to be "futile."

The very first U.S. court case to deal with the issue of end-of-life care was the matter of *In re Quinlan*, a 1976 New Jersey state court case. Quinlan became the first icon of the modern "right to die" movement, although her Catholic family remained true to their church's teachings and did not engage in actual euthanasia or mercy killing. Nevertheless, euthanasia and "right to die" advocates used this opportunity to advance the idea of Living Wills, by which citizens could authorize their own end-of-life wishes, such as the removal of artificial life support or food and water.

Karen Ann Quinlan

On April 15, 1975, Karen Ann Quinlan, only 21, collapsed, stopped breathing, and slipped into a coma. She had just arrived home from a party where her friends reported that she took prescription drugs and drank alcohol after not eating for several days. Doctors were able to save her life, but she suffered severe brain damage and fell into what doctors diagnosed as a persistent vegetative state (PVS). Karen Ann was thought to be unable to breathe without a mechanical device and she was unable to eat without a feeding tube.

After months with no progress, Karen Ann's family saw no hope for their adopted daughter's recovery and they did not want to keep her alive artificially. Her father, who had been appointed guardian, asked the doctors to remove Karen's ventilator, but the hospital refused after being warned that prosecutors could bring homicide charges against them. Karen Ann's doctors refused to remove her life support without a court order to protect them.

As a result, Karen Ann's family went to state court seeking legal protection for the hospital to remove their daughter's ventilator. They won their case and, after receiving their protective court order, the doctors removed Karen Ann's artificial life support.

> *Quinlan ... became one of the earliest American symbols of a patient's "right to die" by refusing medical treatment and artificial life support in order to die "with dignity and grace."*

The Outcome

Karen Ann's ventilator was removed in 1976; however, she surprised everyone and did not die, but began breathing on her own. Karen Ann continued to breath on her own for nine years while living in a New Jersey nursing home. She continued to be fed through a feeding tube and died naturally of pneumonia in 1985.

Karen Ann's parents, while wanting to remove her artificial breathing machine, never considered asking that their daughter's feeding tube be removed. Instead they honored their religious belief that providing basic food and water should be considered "ordinary care", not "extraordinary medical care." If she continued to be fed, God was still able to determine when Karen Ann would die.

Quinlan, despite staying alive and continuing to breathe on her own after her ventilator was removed, became one of the earliest American symbols of a patient's "right to die" by refusing medical treatment and artificial life support in order to die "with dignity and grace," as those who advocate euthanasia describe such deaths.

The Court Decision

The New Jersey Supreme Court's unanimous decision to permit Karen Ann's ventilator to be removed was widely interpreted by those promoting euthanasia as sanctioning a "right to die" for the terminally ill or, in Quinlan's case, for the severely disabled.

In its decision, the New Jersey Supreme Court cited to *Roe v. Wade*, which had been decided by the U.S. Supreme Court only three years earlier and had established that every person has a general constitutional "right to privacy" with regard to medical issues. The New Jersey Supreme Court ruled that this "right to privacy" was "broad enough to encompass a patient's decision to decline medical treatment under certain circumstances in much the same way as it is broad enough to encompass a woman's decision to terminate pregnancy. . . ."

The court held that a competent patient has a constitutional right to choose whether to accept or discontinue life-prolonging medical treatment. Since Quinlan was no longer competent to make this choice for herself, and she had not made this choice while she was still competent, the court ruled that her incompetence was not an acceptable basis for depriving her of a constitutional right to refuse medical treatment and die. Therefore, the court permitted her guardian to make that decision on her behalf. . . .

It is ironic that a case in which the court specifically said the issue was not euthanasia was, nevertheless, used by "right to die" advocates to begin their promotion of voluntary euthanasia through Living Wills.

Whose Right to Choose?

The decision to terminate life at both ends of existence is always cast as a "right to choose." However, it is generally not the person who will die who makes the choice. Mothers make the choice for their unborn babies. Karen Ann Quinlan's parents, doctors and the courts made the choice for her, although, in her case, their choice, although unintended, allowed her to continue living.

In order to vindicate Karen Ann's right to privacy, which she never knew she had, the court held that her father, as guardian, should make that choice for her, just as a pregnant woman makes that choice for her unborn child when deciding to have an abortion. No consideration was given by the New Jersey court to a situation where a guardian and the rest of the patient's family, or even the patient herself, might disagree. That was not the issue before this court, since the whole family was in agreement—that is everyone in the family who was competent to speak, which did not include Karen Ann. No one knew what her decision would have been.

Nancy Cruzan

The case of *Cruzan v. Director of Missouri Dep't of Health* took the end-of-life issue one step farther down the road toward active euthanasia. The Cruzan family wanted to remove their daughter's food and water (ordinary care) rather than artificial life support (extraordinary care). The Court's decision in favor of death by dehydration and starvation was made in 1990. Nancy Cruzan of necessity (since she was provided with no food or water) died 11 days after her feeding tube was removed, on the day after Christmas.

In 1983, 25-year-old Nancy Cruzan lost control of her car and was thrown face down in a ditch. She was discovered by emergency medical technicians with no vital signs, but was resuscitated. This single car accident had left Nancy's brain without oxygen for at least 14 minutes.

Although medical personnel on the scene were able to restore her breathing and heartbeat, Nancy sustained severe brain damage and lapsed into an unconscious state. Within a month, doctors determined that she was in a persistent vegetative state (pvs) with no chance to improve. She was kept alive by a feeding tube and constant medical care, but with no extraordinary artificial life support.

Removing Her Feeding Tube

In May of 1987, four years after Nancy's accident, the Cruzan family, seeing no hope of recovery, requested that her feeding tube be removed in order to cause her death. The hospital refused, just as doctors had initially refused to remove Karen Ann Quinlan's ventilator. Nancy's parents went to court to request a court order protecting the doctors.

Nancy had no written Living Will to indicate what her end of life wishes would be. When the United States Supreme Court determined that "clear and convincing" evidence of Nancy's own wishes would be needed in order to remove her food and water, her family regrouped and solicited several of Nancy's co-workers to testify that Nancy had told them she would not want to live in a disabled condition. The court accepted this testimony as "clear and convincing" evidence.

The majority decision of the U.S. Supreme Court held [in the case of Nancy Cruzan] that a competent adult has a Fourteenth Amendment "liberty" interest in not being forced to undergo unwanted medical procedures.

After seven years of litigation, including involvement by the United States Supreme Court, Nancy's family prevailed. Her feeding tube was removed on December 14, 1990, and she died of dehydration and starvation on the day after Christmas.

This situation was unlike what happened to Karen Ann Quinlan. When Karen Ann's doctors removed her artificial breathing machine, she was able to continue breathing on her own and continued to live for nine more years. Since Karen was still being provided with food and water, she was able to survive for another decade until God's natural time for her death arrived. Nancy, on the other hand, was no longer provided with food and water. Therefore, she was physically unable to continue living for more than a few days. . . .

The Decision

The United States Supreme Court ruled that in attempting to determine the wishes of an incompetent patient, such as Nancy Cruzan, the first question to ask is whether the patient had previously expressed clear wishes either (1) to refuse medical treatment under the circumstances as they existed in the incompetent state (a Living Will) or (2) to designate some other person to make a decision for her in the event of her incapacity (a Designation of Health Care Surrogate).

The majority decision of the U.S. Supreme Court held that a competent adult has a Fourteenth Amendment "liberty" interest in not being forced to undergo unwanted medical procedures. . . .

The outcome in the Cruzan case, which favored death over life, again highlighted the "right to die" movement, which was then already promoting mercy killing in the United States. Americans were even more forcibly alerted to the fact that they needed to document their end-of-life wishes before they became disabled or incompetent. Living Wills were aggressively promoted by America's euthanasia advocates as a means through which individuals could indicate ahead of time that they wanted to refuse certain types of medical treatment, including food and water, if they should become incompetent or otherwise unable to speak for themselves. The use of Living Wills became ever more common in America in the wake of the Cruzan case, although they tended to encourage a choice for death rather than life in adverse medical situations.

Estelle Browning

The 1990 case of *In re Guardianship of Browning*, which was decided the same year as the Cruzan case, was an important Florida state court decision that established a "right to die" through refusing artificial nutrition and hydration, as well as extraordinary medical treatment. It involved Living Wills and the right to refuse, not only treatment, but food and water as well, in order to make sure that death would occur. This case could be characterized as establishing a "right to suicide."

The execution of a Living Will allows caregivers to withhold food and water, as well as artificial life support, from an incapacitated person even when death is not imminent.

Mrs. Estelle Browning, an 86-year-old Floridian, suffered a stoke in 1986 and became unable to communicate. Unlike Nancy Cruzan and Karen Ann Quinlan, Mrs. Browning had a Living Will in place stating that she did not want to be kept alive by artificial means if she ever became ill, nor did she want to be fed via a feeding tube.

Nevertheless, the Florida nursing home in which she was residing refused to remove Mrs. Browning's feeding tube and cause her death. Mrs. Browning's cousin, her closest relative, engaged the legal services of a Florida "right to die" attorney, George Felos, to obtain a court order requiring the nursing home to follow Mrs. Browning's Living Will and remove her feeding tube.

The Outcome

Mrs. Browning was the only prominent end-of-life litigant who had actually drafted a Living Will before surviving an incapacitating stroke. She stated in her Living Will that she did not want to be kept alive by artificial means, including a feeding tube. Nevertheless, before her case was concluded, Mrs. Browning died of natural causes in 1989, ironically, the very way she had not chosen in her Living Will. She died at the age of 89 in a Florida nursing home, still being fed through a feeding tube.

Rather than declare Mrs. Browning's case moot following her natural death, the Florida Supreme Court decided to issue a ruling a year later. The court held that the execution of a

Living Will allows caregivers to withhold food and water, as well as artificial life support, from an incapacitated person even when death is not imminent. This decision became an important Florida precedent for the Terri Schiavo case a few years later, even though Mrs. Schiavo, unlike Mrs. Browning, was not terminally ill and had never executed a Living Will.

Terri Schiavo

The *Browning* case set the stage for the most recent and probably most well-known "right to die" case—that of Terri Schiavo, a young Florida woman who was severely brain damaged following a collapse of unknown origin in her home. There were, however, several significant differences in the circumstances of these two Floridians. Terri was physically healthy and could have lived for many more years. She did not have a Living Will or any other written end-of-life or health care document. Her parents, Bob and Mary Schindler and siblings, Bobby and Suzanne, wanted to care for her and provide therapy, but her husband found George Felos, Mrs. Browning's lawyer, and went to court to obtain a death sentence from a civil court.

Terri Schiavo collapsed on February 25, 1990, at the age of 26, while at home with her husband under circumstances that have still not been fully determined. Michael Schiavo, discontinued all therapy and rehabilitation in 1992, after receiving a large medical malpractice award. He instructed Terri's nursing home caregivers not to treat his wife if she became ill. After the nursing home treated her for a life threatening condition against his orders, Michael Schiavo engaged the services of George Felos, the Florida "right to die" attorney who had represented Mrs. Browning.

Michael went to court in 1998 under a new 1997 Florida law that seemed tailored to Terri's situation, allowing a patient diagnosed as being in PVS to be put to death, even without a written document, and to be denied food and water by order of a court. Michael asked Judge George Greer of the Pinellas County Probate Court to order his wife's feeding tube removed and end her life. The court determined that Terri was in a persistent vegetative state, although PVS was misdiagnosed nearly half the time. Terri's parents and siblings, along with their medical experts, consistently challenged Terri's PVS diagnosis, but without success.

A New Legal Standard

The legal standard for ending Terri's life was the *Cruzan* standard of clear and convincing evidence. Michael and two members of his family testified that Terri had told them she would not want to live in a disabled condition. Even though Terri's mother and a friend both testified that she had told them she did not think Karen Ann Quinlan's parents should have removed her life support, the judge ruled there was clear and convincing evidence that Terri would have wanted to die.

> *After 1997, Florida law considered feeding tubes to be medical treatment, like a respirator or heart/lung machine, which patients have a constitutional privacy right to refuse.*

The first court order to discontinue use of her feeding apparatus (which placed liquid nutrition directly into her stomach) and end Terri's life was handed down in 2000. Two more such orders would follow in 2003 and 2005, as Terri's parents and siblings continued their fight to save her life. Terri's parents argued (unsuccessfully at every turn) that (1) Michael had a conflict of interest and should not continue as Terri's guardian since he had entered into a committed relationship with another woman, with whom he had two children, and since he would financially profit from his wife's death, (2) that Terri would not want to die by starvation and dehydration, which violated her Catholic faith as well as her personal feelings, (3) that Michael was refusing to provide rehabilitative therapy for Terri, which might have improved her condition, and (4) that Terri was not in a persistent vegetative state (PVS), but needed further medical testing to determine if she was in a minimally conscious state (MCS), which would not have permitted the court to remove her food and water under Florida law.

Terri's feeding apparatus was finally discontinued for the last time on March 18, 2005 and she died 13 days later on March 31, still appearing to recognize her family and to be aware of what was going on around her. . . .

The Decision

After 1997, Florida law considered feeding tubes to be medical treatment, like a respirator or heart/lung machine, which patients have a constitutional privacy right to refuse. Florida law also provides that if a patient is incompetent, has been diagnosed as being in a persistent vegetative state (PVS), and does not have a Living Will or Advance Health Care Directive, the patient's guardian may go to court to have the patient's feeding tube removed thereby causing the patient's death even if the patient is not terminally ill. . . .

Terri's case has permitted Florida nursing homes and hospitals to more easily end the lives of the disabled and elderly, based on a PVS diagnosis, even when patients have not indicated their end-of-life wishes in writing and are not terminally ill. Families or guardians only need to state that death would have been the patient's wish, even when other family members might disagree. This trend is spreading to other states whose legislatures are also enacting laws favoring death over life. Judges and doctors, as well as some families, use a "quality of life" standard to determine that a patient would no longer wish to live, rather than allowing God to determine the patient's time of death.

Assisted Suicide Laws

Oregon became the first state in the nation to enact legislation allowing physician-assisted suicide under nearly any circumstances. In 2006, in the case of *Gonzales v. Oregon*, the United States Supreme Court upheld Oregon's radical "right to die" law as constitutional.

The federal Controlled Substances Act (CSA) was enacted in 1970 to govern the distribution of certain substances. It requires doctors to register for the right to distribute particular medications. The CSA also gives the U.S. Attorney General power to deny, suspend or revoke a doctor's registration that would be "inconsistent with the public interest."

Oregon later enacted the state's Oregon Death With Dignity Act (ODWDA), giving doctors the right to prescribe medicines the patient intended to use to commit suicide. The U.S. Attorney General issued an Interpretive Rule stating that the use of prescriptions for physician-assisted suicide was not a "legitimate medical purpose." This meant that if an Oregon doctor prescribed medication so that a patient could commit suicide, the doctor would be in violation of the CSA.

The Court Case

The State of Oregon and other individuals sued the federal government to prevent enforcement of the federal CSA against doctors who took advantage of the ODWDA in order to assist their patients to commit suicide. The United States Supreme Court held that the U.S. Attorney General's Interpretive Rule was invalid and a majority of Justices upheld Oregon's practice of assisted suicide as permitted by the ODWDA.

The Court ruled that The Controlled Substance Act did not authorize the U.S. Attorney General to prohibit doctors from prescribing regulated drugs for use in physician-assisted suicide. Their rationale was that to allow the U.S. Attorney General to enforce its Interpretive Rule to invalidate the Oregon statute would violate state's rights and permit the federal government to intrude on issues of life and death determined by the States. Of course, this ruling was the exact opposite of the ruling in *Roe v. Wade*, which allowed the federal government to overrule state laws prohibiting abortion, but no one seemed to mind that contradictory detail.

The Attorney General's Interpretive Rule, which had stated that physician-assisted suicide was not a legitimate medical purpose for the use of controlled substances, was declared by the Court to be invalid. This decision now allows individuals in Oregon and in any state that cares to enact such legislation to engage in physician-assisted suicide.

2

Terminally Ill People Should Have the Right to Die

Scott Mendelson

Scott Mendelson is a physician and author of the book Beyond Alzheimer's: How to Avoid the Modern Epidemic of Dementia.

Many people who are struggling with debilitating and terminal illnesses must deal with excruciating and unrelenting pain, as well as the loss of their autonomy and the ability to care for themselves. Outside assistance and pain medication may not be enough to mitigate their suffering, and such individuals often feel that their life is not bearable under such conditions. This kind of suffering is not meaningful or noble, as many religious teachings would maintain. It is cruel and pathological to force people to endure a painful, tortured existence in which there is no hope for relief but that ultimately brought by death. It is time for society to grant the right to die, with safeguards in place to make sure the option is used appropriately.

In our society there continues to be a controversy about the right of an individual to end their own life when living becomes emotionally and physically unbearable for them. This may be the case when a medical problem leads a person to lose everything they feel necessary to continue a dignified, meaningful life.

It is not uncommon for people in the end stages of catastrophically disabling neurological illnesses, such as Amyotrophic Lateral Sclerosis (ALS) or Huntington's Disease, to desire a controlled and painless end to their existence. In other cases, loss of function coupled with unbearable disfiguration due to cancer, trauma, neurofibromatosis, or other conditions leads a person to feel that no form of meaningful, acceptable existence is possible. For others, it is never ending, intractable, excruciating pain that makes existence unbearable. For too long we have forced human beings to suffer under the primitive religious notion that it is "God's" decision and not our own to end life.

Safeguards are written into the Oregon law to prevent an individual who is psychiatrically ill from making an ill-conceived and irrational decision to end their life.

The Meaning of Suffering

The subtext of the notion that it is "God's" decision to end life tormented by suffering has always been that suffering is meaningful, and that God has a purpose for it. Few would argue against the common understanding that adversity ennobles the mind. Loss, disappointment, pain, defeat, and failure are the great teachers of humanity. They lead us to seek the comfort and guidance of others. We experience consolation, and we learn to give such consolation to others. We learn that to persevere through pain and defeat can bring rewards far sweeter than they might have been had they been more easily and less painfully achieved. Pain and adversity teaches us patience, humility, empathy, grace, courage, and hope. It teaches us what it means to be one among other human beings. Indeed, it may be the basis if not the prerequisite for love in its most mature form. However, on what basis do we force an individual to continue to suffer an excruciatingly painful existence in which there is no longer any hope, comfort, or meaning?

Some argue that to allow people the right to end their life when and as they choose is the first step down a road to nihilism and wholesale suicide. However, experience shows that this is not the case. Where physician assisted suicide is legal, such as in my own home state of Oregon, those who have successfully pursued access to medications to end their life most often choose to go on living. The sense of control and choice they experience gives them the courage and peace of mind to see it out a little longer. There is also an unfounded concern that allowing an individual to take their life under such circumstances is a slippery slope to encouraging or compelling people to take their own lives. However, aside from being unfounded, this concern is easily resolved. We must simply prohibit encouragement and compulsion!

Pain and Personal Choice

There are some who argue against assisted suicide because they are under the impression that modern medical science is capable of treating and relieving all forms of physical pain. This, unfortunately, is untrue. There are forms of physical pain that do not respond to medication. People who suffer pain resistant to medication are sometimes helped by pumping pain medication directly around their spinal cord. Others are helped by surgery that cuts pain pathways in their brain, or by implantation of electrodes that alter brain function. But for some people not even those extreme measures bring relief from pain. No matter what is done, some human beings continue to suffer unrelenting, unbearable pain. They should not be forced to endure it.

A final and perhaps more complex question is on what basis would we establish criteria to define the conditions and forms of suffering that might justify suicide. Clearly, there is a possibility that people might choose suicide due to frivolous, temporary, or easily resolved problems. Safeguards are written into the Oregon law to prevent an individual who is psychiatrically ill from making an ill-conceived and irrational decision to end their life. There is also a waiting period to prevent rash or precipitous actions. Common sense dictates that we rule out conditions that are likely to be reversed by treatment.

The current law in Oregon is based on the confirmation of a terminal illness, and not necessarily for intractable pain or loss of meaningful existence. I believe the law would be more humane by allowing for individual variation and personal choice. Whereas Stephen Hawking, through his magnificent life of the mind, has found a means to live a meaningful and productive life with ALS, not everyone with the illness can do so. Nonetheless, Oregon's law is a good one and, for most states, allowing an individual with unmitigated suffering in the context of a terminal illness to seek a physician's help to end their life would be a major step forward.

Religious Arguments

The argument against physician assisted suicide and the right to die is almost entirely a religious one. There are many reasonable religious individuals who see that a just and loving God would forgive any mere human being for finding a peaceful, painless way out of unmitigated misery. I applaud them. On the other hand, for those of us who do not believe in a sugar-coated God that makes all things right in the end, the notion that one should be forced to persist in a painful, unbearable existence, without respite or hope of remedy is cruel, barbaric, and pathological. It is time that our society grows up and grants the right to die.

3

Physician-Assisted Dying Is Ethical

Marcia Angell

Marcia Angell is a physician and the former editor of the New England Journal of Medicine, *as well as a senior lecturer in social medicine at Harvard Medical School.*

Death with Dignity laws—like the one enacted in Oregon in 1994 and the one put before Massachusetts voters in 2012—have many built-in safeguards to ensure that the laws are appropriately used. No one should be able to dictate how much suffering a dying individual must endure, and physician-assisted dying is not about life versus death but rather about the manner and type of death. Critics who say that Death with Dignity laws are open to abuse should study the Oregon law and see how scrupulously it has been applied. Physician-assisted dying is an ethical choice, and doctors should feel good about standing up for the needs of their patients on such an important issue.

Editor's Note: The 2012 Death with Dignity Act in Massachusetts failed to pass by a slim margin: 49 percent yes to 51 percent no.

On Nov. 6 [2012], in addition to weighing in on the crucial political contests, Massachusetts voters will decide whether physicians may provide a dying patient with medication to bring about an earlier, more peaceful death if the patient chooses. On the ballot will be a Death with Dignity Act that is virtually identical to the law that has been in effect in Oregon for many years. If it passes, it will legalize physician-assisted dying, sometimes called aid in dying. (These terms are favored over the older term, physician-assisted suicide, because they distinguish it from the typical suicide in which a healthy person chooses death over life; here the patient is near death from natural causes anyway, and merely chooses the timing and manner of an inevitable death.)

There are a host of safeguards. First, the Act applies only to adults who are able to make their own decisions. It cannot be used through advance directives, nor by people with limited decision-making capacity. Second, the patient must have a terminal illness, with a life expectancy of no more than six months, as determined by at least two physicians. In addition, the patient must make two oral requests for medication to hasten death, separated by at least 15 days, and one written request, with two witnesses. By definition, the patient must be capable of swallowing the medication—usually barbiturates dissolved in a full glass of liquid—which ensures that it is voluntary. The law does not permit euthanasia, that is, the injection of a lethal medication by a physician or anyone else. If a physician believes a psychiatric condition is impairing the patient's judgment, the doctor must refer him or her to a psychiatrist or other counselor. No physician is required to participate in assisted dying; he or she may refuse for any reason whatsoever. This is a choice, not a requirement, for both patients and physicians.

Refuting the Law's Opponents

Last December, at its interim meeting, the Massachusetts Medical Society reaffirmed its long-standing opposition to physician-assisted dying—finding it "inconsistent with the physician's role as healer and health care provider," in the words of President Lynda Young. I will here discuss this and other arguments often made by physician opponents, and explain why I believe they are wrong, both medically and ethically.

Physicians are only healers. This sees the physician's role too narrowly and abstractly. Yes, it is all very well to say that physicians should be healers, but suppose healing is not possible? When death is imminent and dying patients find their suffering unbearable, then the physician's role should shift from healing to relieving suffering in accord with the patient's wishes. This is not a matter of life versus death, but about the manner of dying, and it's not primarily about doctors, but about patients.

No law works absolutely perfectly, but [the Oregon Death with Dignity Act] seems to come about as close as possible.

Physicians should never participate in taking life. Doctors who believe this do not usually object to withdrawing life-sustaining treatment, such as a mechanical ventilator, if requested by a patient or proxy. But they believe that writing a prescription is more active, hence unethical. Here again, this argument focuses too much on physicians and not enough on patients. If we look instead at the patient's role, we see that assisted dying requires purposeful actions on the part of the patient, whereas a mechanical ventilator could be disconnected from an unconscious patient. Even some doctors who believe assisted dying is sometimes warranted think they should not write the prescription, but outsource it to someone else. This is a form of abandonment, in which doctors prize their self-image above the patient's needs.

Depression and the Slippery Slope Argument

Patients who request assisted dying may be suffering from treatable depression. The diagnosis of depression is difficult because the symptoms overlap with those of terminal illness, and dying naturally produces sadness. Moreover, there are no good studies of the effectiveness of therapy in this setting. Nevertheless, the act requires physicians to refer patients for counseling if they believe a patient's judgment is impaired by depression or another psychiatric condition, and that is a common reason doctors give for denying requests in Oregon.

Permitting assisted dying will put us on a "slippery slope," leading to abuses, such as using the law for patients who are not terminally ill or who are especially vulnerable—for example, the uninsured. The best answers come from Oregon, where the law has been used sparingly (most requests are refused) and exactly as intended. Assisted dying there has accounted for 596 deaths over 14 years, only 0.2 percent of all deaths in the most recent year. Most patients were suffering from metastatic cancer, and the prognosis was clear. Far from being vulnerable, they were relatively affluent, well-educated, and well-insured, and nearly all were receiving hospice care at the time of their request. About a third who requested medication did not use it, but kept it at hand because it provided peace of mind. No law works absolutely perfectly, but this one seems to come about as close as possible.

Physical and Existential Suffering

Good palliative care can relieve all suffering, so permitting assisted dying is unnecessary. Probably most dying patients, even when suffering greatly, would choose to live as long as possible. That courage and grace should be protected and honored, and we should put every effort into treating their symptoms. (Palliative care in Oregon is among the best in the country.) But not all suffering can be relieved. Most pain can, but other symptoms can be harder to deal with—symptoms such as weakness, loss of control of bodily functions, shortness of breath, and nausea—and the drugs to treat them often produce side effects that are as debilitating as the problems they treat. Even worse for many patients is the existential suffering. They know that their condition will grow worse day after day until their deaths, that their course is inexorably downhill, and they find it meaningless to soldier on. Why should anyone—the state, the medical profession, or anyone else—presume to tell someone else how much suffering they must endure while dying? Doctors should stand with their patients, not against them.

4

Physician-Assisted Dying Is Not Ethical

Barbara A. Rockett

Barbara A. Rockett is a physician at Newton-Wellesley Hospital in Newton, Massachusetts, and former president of the Massachusetts Medical Society.

When people become physicians, they typically take the Hippocratic Oath, a pledge that guides the ethical practice of medicine. The oath specifies that the primary duty of a physician is to "first do no harm," and it also specifically says that a doctor shall "give no deadly medicine to anyone if asked." Physician-assisted suicide is in direct conflict with the Hippocratic Oath, and it represents the abandonment of the vow that doctors make to care for patients and promote their welfare. Physician-assisted suicide is not death with dignity; it is unethical and it undermines not just the doctor-patient relationship but the very commitment that physicians make to life and healing.

Physicians, in their care of patients, must establish a physician-patient relationship based on mutual trust and respect to be able to render the best care to their patients. Centuries ago the physician Hippocrates wrote the Hippocratic Oath, which many of us took when we became physicians and guides us in the ethical practice of medicine. It states that when treating patients, physicians will "First do no harm." It goes on to state that "I will give no deadly medicine to anyone if asked nor suggest any such counsel." Physician-assisted suicide is in direct conflict with this statement which, when followed, has protected the patient, physician, society and the family, and at the same time has committed doctors to compassion and human dignity.

As a practicing physician, I have cared for many patients throughout their lives, extending through to their last days of life. Their needs must be honored and their dignity preserved, which might require alleviation of pain, treatment of depression if it exists, as well as support for them and their families. Palliative or hospice care must be offered when appropriate.

I was impressed with the courage and fortitude of many in wheelchairs and on canes and on crutches who might require this care and who testified before the Judiciary Committee at the [Massachusetts] State House in opposition to physician-assisted suicide. We physicians must assure them that we will always be there to protect them and administer the care that they might require.

The AMA opposes physician-assisted suicide as antithetical to the role of the physician as healer.

Saving Money Instead of Patients

It has been demonstrated that the highest cost of medical care exists in the last six months of life. We must resist advocating for physician-assisted suicide as an alternative to spending money caring for these patients. We as physicians must avoid the so-called slippery slope of attempting to save money by doing less for our patients rather than rendering the proper care to them. To substitute physician-assisted suicide for care represents an abandonment of the patient by the physician.

Massachusetts has had the outstanding reputation of training medical students, residents, and fellows in the care of patients. Let's not put a blemish on that reputation by advocating for physician-assisted suicide.

The present initiative does not require that the physician be present when the patient takes the medicine, so there is no guarantee that the patient will ever receive it.

One of the most difficult and often inadequate determinations that a physician has to make is the attempt to predict when a patient might die. An example of this occurred when my husband, a neurosurgeon, saw a patient who had been operated on by the renowned neurosurgeon Dr. Harvey Cushing for the most malignant type of brain tumor. The surgery was followed by radiation therapy. He was told that he had six months to live, so he spent his savings doing all the things he had hoped to do in life. When the six months were over, he could not get a job, he could not get insurance, and he was very upset that he was given a bad prognosis. That was 40 years before my husband saw him. Thinking that the diagnosis might have been incorrect, pathologists reviewed the slides and applied all the modern techniques, only to find that the original diagnosis was absolutely correct. He did, in fact, have the most malignant type of brain tumor. Although this is a rare case and illustrates the exception to the rule, it shows that exceptions can occur and that there are outliers to the statistics.

American Medical Association Statement

More than 75 percent of the physician members of the Massachusetts Medical Society have voted to oppose physician-assisted suicide. Since their meeting in 1999, the members of the American Medical Association [AMA] have voted to oppose physician-assisted suicide and have been consistent in their opposition, stating, "The AMA opposes physician-assisted suicide as antithetical to the role of the physician as healer. We are committed to providing the best end-of-life care." At a meeting in 2003, the AMA went on to state, "Physician-assisted suicide is fundamentally incompatible with the physician's role as healer, would be difficult or impossible to control, and would impose serious societal risks."

The Massachusetts Board of Registration in Medicine has imposed a requirement on physicians seeking to be licensed in Massachusetts that they must complete a course in end-of-life care and another in opioid prescribing. These courses educate the physician in the compassionate, considerate, and supportive care that must be offered to patients at the end of life. Reasonable prescribing of opioids should be offered only when necessary and should not be substituted for other needs such as treatment of depression.

Undermining the Doctor-Patient Relationship

Dr. Lonnie Bristow, former president of the AMA, has made the following statement: "There is a great deal of concern in this nation about the issue of physician-assisted suicide. It is important, in fact, incumbent among the American Medical Association to spell out its position on this important issue. Just what is our position? Simply put, we oppose it. We believe that physician-assisted suicide is unethical, it is fundamentally inconsistent with the pledge that physicians make to devote themselves to healing and to life. We believe laws sanctioning physician-assisted suicide serve to undermine the foundation of the patient-physician relationship, which is grounded in the patient's trust that the physician is working wholeheartedly for the patient's health and welfare."

Physician-assisted suicide has been falsely advertised as death with dignity. Believe me, there is nothing dignified about suicide.

5

Patients Who Lack Hope Need Advocates, Not Suicide Help

Rosemarie Jackowski

Rosemarie Jackowski is an advocacy journalist and peace activist who is the author of the book Banned in Vermont. *Her writing frequently appears at VTDigger.org, a statewide news website dedicated to coverage of Vermont politics, consumer affairs, business, and public policy.*

No matter what anyone says, there are no safeguards that can ensure assisted suicide laws will not be abused. The disabled, the elderly, and others who are especially vulnerable may be pressured to end their lives to save money on expensive medical care or to simply make life easier for their families. Additionally, some people who consider assisted suicide do so because they are in less-than-ideal situations that could be corrected. Substandard nursing homes and inadequate pain control are just two examples of situations that can lead patients to despair. Having effective health-care advocates is essential to protecting vulnerable patients and ensuring that end-of-life needs are anticipated and met so patients don't feel their best or only option is assisted suicide.

The "assisted suicide bill" does exactly what it is designed *not* to do. It will eliminate choice for the most vulnerable. Unintended consequences are sure to follow. We need more, not fewer, rights. Government-approved suicide as an end-of-life option does not give more rights—in reality it takes them away.

Some legislators promise "safeguards." There are no safeguards that can ensure that there will not be abuse. Some of the most vulnerable will be pressured to end it all for the convenience and sometimes for the financial benefit of others. Patients will be unduly influenced into giving in to family members. Many elderly/disabled have loving supportive families. It is those who do not who are at the highest risk. There is no way that abuse can be prevented. Imagine being isolated with caregivers—Stockholm syndrome [a well-documented syndrome in which captives come to identify with their captors].

Assisted Suicide Laws Hurt Rather than Help

The assisted suicide law will deprive many of choice. Recent history shows that more than 300 cases of reported abuse of the disabled/elderly have been ignored by the state. This is evidence that the state cannot protect the vulnerable. The assisted suicide law will add another layer of risk. It will make things worse.

It can be argued that there are some justifications for suicide. That may be true, but belief in the infallibility of a diagnosis is not a valid reason.

Prejudice cloaked in good intentions is still prejudice. Why is the law limited to the most vulnerable, the disabled, the elderly? If suicide is a movement that will benefit society, open it up to everyone. The devaluing of the elderly and disabled is now an accepted fact of life and death. If this law did not show prejudice against the most vulnerable, it would be written to include everyone—young and old, healthy and sick. Sometimes the young and healthy would chose to end it all.

For those pressured to die, there will be no choice. Behind closed doors in private, who will be there to protect them? Elder abuse is a major hidden problem. Talk to anyone in a nursing home—give them anonymity, and they will tell all.

The Need for Advocates

Recently, a friend was searching for a way out . . . suicide. He was not in physical pain. He was not terminally ill. His problem was that he was in a nursing home and the conditions there were not good. What he needed was a health care advocate—someone to advocate for him. The need for health care advocates is one of the biggest issues of our time. Families are dispersed and distant. Often the elderly are abandoned. Friends die. Suddenly a nursing home is the only option. There have been two reported murders in local nursing homes in recent years. No one can estimate how many murders go unreported. Isolation, neglect and poor living conditions are other important issues.

It can be argued that there are some justifications for suicide. That may be true, but belief in the infallibility of a diagnosis is not a valid reason. Some doctors and hospitals have already announced that they will not participate in this type of death process.

Asking the Right Questions

The assisted suicide bill is the wrong answer to the wrong question. The important question is not the length of time left. "*. . . Over the years I've learned that my patients are people who can live an entire lifetime in six months or a year. What they do with this time represents a much higher quality of life than that enjoyed by 'normal' people who are caught up in the trivia of day-to-day, and not really focused on what is important*" [writes] Keith Black, MD, author of "Brain Surgeon."

The question that we should be asking is "how can we improve life and death for all?" There are three unmet needs that should be addressed by the Legislature.

First, health care must be made available to all. Universal, comprehensive single payer that includes dental, vision and long-term care is the answer.

Second, the alleviation of pain must be considered. Ethics require that everything scientifically possible should be done to eliminate suffering. It is usually possible to do that without killing the patient.

Third, and most important of all, those at high risk must be protected. There is only one way to do that. We must set up a system of health care advocates. This does not have to cost taxpayers a lot of money. A system based on volunteers could work. The main qualification would be compassion and the pledge to honor privacy.

Will we soon see Grandpa set adrift on an ice floe on the shore of Lake Champlain? There must be a better way.

6

Aid in Dying Is Different from Assisted Suicide

Barbara Coombs Lee

Barbara Coombs Lee is president of the end-of-life choice advo-cacy and support group, Compassion & Choices (formerly the Hemlock Society), and was a chief petitioner of the first-in-the-nation Oregon Death with Dignity Act.

Those who advocate for end-of-life choice in dying feel very strongly about the issue. But they feel just as strongly that as-sisted suicide should never be permitted. In several important ways, the difference between aid-in-dying and assisted suicide is very stark; yet laws against assisted suicide have often been mis-interpreted to mean that a dying person cannot ask their doctor for medications that will hasten their death peacefully. That is not the intent of such laws, whose primary purpose is to protect vulnerable people from undue outside influence. Assisted suicide is and should remain a crime. Aid-in-dying is a kindness. The distinction between the two is plain to anyone who looks closely enough.

This week [May 2010] William Melchert-Dinkel, a former nurse from Faribault, Minnesota, appeared in court on charges of assisting the suicide of a British man and Canadian woman. He stands accused of instructing and coaxing these young people and others in Internet suicide chat rooms to kill themselves.

Barbara Coombs Lee, "The Crime of Assisting a Suicide," *Huffington Post*, May 26, 2010. Copyright © Barbara Coombs Lee 2010. All rights reserved. Reproduced with permis-sion.

Reporters have been calling [national end-of-life advocacy organization] Compassion & Choices for comment, perhaps with the expectation that we would not condemn the alleged behavior. Nothing could be further from the truth.

Let's be clear. Our movement for end-of-life choice does not condone assisted suicide, and it never has. When we drafted the Oregon Death with Dignity Act in 1994 we were careful to preserve and maintain the felony of assisting a suicide. That law protects Oregonians with poor mental health and disordered thinking from anyone who would encourage and facilitate their attempts to harm themselves. Laws against assisted suicide are good laws that should stay on the books in every state where they appear.

The History of Assisted Suicide Law

History of assisted suicide laws is instructive. A wave of reform legislation passed through the United States in the 1970's to repeal ancient statutes making suicide and attempted suicide a crime. Those misguided laws hearkened back to feudal England, where citizens were deemed to "belong" to the king, and killing oneself amounted to destruction of property obligated to the crown. By the twentieth century, advances in psychiatry demonstrated that self-destructive thoughts called for mental health intervention, not criminal prosecution. So legislatures transformed the crime of "suicide" into the crime of "assisting a suicide" to punish the aiding and abetting of harmful behavior of the mentally ill. It's a crime to shout "jump, jump" to a distressed person clinging to a high window ledge. It's a crime to goad depressed teenagers into playing Russian roulette, or pretend to join them in a suicide pact. People who commit these crimes should be tried and punished accordingly for assisting, or attempting to assist a suicide.

These laws do have a problem, however. The problem is lawyers, doctors and other people have made overly broad assumptions about them. People have assumed assisted suicide laws prevent dying patients from asking their doctors for life-ending medication they could take if the suffering in their dying became unbearable. They assume the physician would be "assisting a suicide" even though rational dying patients are not "suicidal" and no American physician has ever been successfully prosecuted for empowering a dying patient with the means to humane and peaceful passing. Doctors who acknowledge their patients' imminent death and accede to their thoughtful request are providing aid in dying, not assisted suicide.

> *Suicide is an expression of despair and futility; aid in dying is an affirmation of a person's dignity and rational self-determination.*

Stark Opposites

The contrast between aid in dying, in which a knowledgeable, merciful physician gives his elderly, dying patient the means to halt end-of-life suffering—and assisted suicide, in which a malicious predator seeks out and victimizes physically healthy, mentally ill teens—could not be more clear.

Consider the stark opposites outlined by Dr. James Lieberman in *Psychiatric News*, a publication of the American Psychiatric Association:

- The suicidal patient has no terminal illness but wants to die; the aid in dying patient has a terminal illness and wants to live.

- Suicides bring shock and tragedy to families and friends; aid in dying deaths are peaceful and supported by loved ones.

- Suicides are secretive and often impulsive and violent. Aid in Dying is planned; it changes only the

The Right to Die

timing of imminent death in a minor way, but adds control in a major and socially approved way.

- Suicide is an expression of despair and futility; aid in dying is an affirmation of a person's dignity and rational self-determination.

In short, suicide is the self-destructive impulse of a person who has every reason and ability to live. Aid in dying is the self-affirming decision of a person who cannot choose to live, and can only choose the manner of an imminent death.

The charges against Melchart-Dinkel relate to the suicides of Mark Drybrough, 32, who hanged himself at his home in Coventry, England, in 2005, and Nadia Kajouji, an 18-year-old from Brampton, Ontario, who drowned in a river in Ottawa where she was studying at Carleton University. According to the charges, Melchert-Dinkel used Yahoo and Google chats to instruct the victims how to tie and hang a noose. He allegedly encouraged them to use a webcam so he could witness the suicides. He admitted to enticing 10 or 11 individuals into suicide pacts, and assisting several more than the two for which he is charged, in killing themselves.

Who can read these charges without feeling shock and disgust and knowing a crime has been committed?

Crime vs. Kindness

Contrast these horrors with the elderly cancer patient, who gallantly fights the disease for years and finally acknowledges the approaching end, as cancer continues to ravage and degrade the ailing body. This person's doctor thoroughly assesses the dismal prognosis and the rational nature of his patient's request. After a period of waiting, watching and weighing the magnitude and course of suffering, this patient asks his loved ones to support his wish and be with him at his passing. At an appointed time they gather at his bedside, singing, praying and affirming their love as he drinks the life-ending medication his doctor has prescribed.

Who can read this description without feeling sympathy and knowing, somewhere deep inside where our humanity longs for freedom and dignity, that such a death is sad, as all death is, but it is not criminal?

The two situations are so different, it is impossible to use the same phrase to name them. Indeed, the crime is assisted suicide. The kindness is aid in dying.

7

The Death with Dignity Movement Is Gaining Acceptance Nationwide

Susan Haigh

Associated Press journalist Susan Haigh is a political writer and statehouse reporter in Hartford, Connecticut.

The 2012 Death with Dignity ballot measure in Massachusetts may have failed by a narrow margin, but it brought significant attention to right-to-die issues and sparked a national dialogue on the topic. Bills that would legalize physician-assisted suicide are currently being considered in several different states, and other bills related to the issue are popping up in statehouses across the country. Opponents say that the national push is being fueled by end-of-life advocacy groups, such as Compassion & Choices, rather than from any sort of grassroots movement on the state level. The large number of baby boomers—people born between 1946 and 1964—who are growing old has also helped push the Death with Dignity movement into the national spotlight.

A push for the legalization of physician-assisted suicide is under way in a half-dozen states where proponents say they see strong support for allowing doctors to prescribe mentally competent, dying individuals with the medications needed to end their own lives.

The large number of baby boomers facing end-of-life issues themselves is seen to have made the issue more prominent in recent years. Groups such as Compassion & Choices, a national end-of-life advocacy organization, have been working to advance the cause.

Advocates received a boost from last year's [2012] ballot question in Massachusetts on whether to allow physicians to help the terminally ill die. Although the vote failed, it helped to spark a national discussion, said Mickey MacIntyre, chief program officer for Compassion & Choices.

"The Massachusetts initiative lifted the consciousness of the nation and in particular the Northeast region to this issue that there are other alternatives patients and their families should have an opportunity to access," MacIntyre said.

Bills legalizing assisted suicide are being considered in Connecticut, Vermont, New Jersey, Kansas and Hawaii—and in Massachusetts, where proponents decided to resume their efforts after the public vote, according to the National Conference of State Legislatures, which tracks legislative trends. There are also bills related to the issue under consideration in New Hampshire, New York, Arizona and Montana.

Thirty-four states prohibit assisted suicide outright. Seven others, including Massachusetts, banned it through legal precedent.

In Connecticut, which has banned the practice since 1969, a group of lawmakers said Tuesday [February 5, 2013] that the legislature's first public hearing on the subject would probably be held this month. At least two bills on the issue have so far been proposed in this year's session of the Connecticut legislature.

If the General Assembly votes to legalize the practice, it would be the first state legislature to do so.

States Have Varying Laws

Oregon and Washington have passed right-to-die laws, but they did so through voter referendums. Montana's Supreme Court has ruled that the practice of physicians helping terminally ill patients could be considered part of medical treatments. Thirty-four states prohibit assisted suicide outright. Seven others, including Massachusetts, banned it through legal precedent.

Opponents claim the initiatives in Connecticut are being pushed only by outside groups like Compassion & Choices.

"There's no grass-roots cry for assisted suicide in the state of Connecticut," said Peter Wolfgang, executive director of the socially conservative Family Institute. "This is mostly an out-of-state organization that has targeted the state of Connecticut. They look at the Northeast and think this is low-hanging fruit: 'We can conduct our social experiments here in the Northeastern United States.'"

In fact, one bill has been filed in Connecticut this year that would establish a mandatory minimum prison term for someone charged with second-degree manslaughter after assisting another person with committing suicide.

A measure dubbed "end of life choices" recently sped through the Vermont Senate Health and Welfare Committee but is expected to face a bumpier ride in the Judiciary Committee. In New Jersey, a bill that would allow doctors to prescribe lethal doses of medication for terminally ill patients wishing to take their own lives cleared an Assembly committee Thursday. That legislation would ultimately be subject to voter approval.

Last November, voters in Massachusetts narrowly defeated a measure legalizing physician-assisted suicide for the terminally ill. Supporters of the concept said they hoped the debate would continue and marked the beginning of a conversation to improve end-of-life care.

Doctors Could Be Prosecuted

In Connecticut, Dr. Gary Blick, a Norwalk physician who specializes in treating patients with HIV and AIDS, said he believes the time is right for state lawmakers to push ahead with this issue. In 2009, he and Dr. Ron Levine, of Greenwich, along with end-of-life advocates, sued to seek a clarification of the state's decades-old ban on assisted suicide, citing concerns about Connecticut doctors being prosecuted for giving medications to their dying patients.

A judge ultimately dismissed the suit, saying it was a matter for the legislature to decide.

The 1969 Connecticut law states that a person who "intentionally causes or aids another person, other than by force, duress or deception, to commit suicide" is guilty of second-degree manslaughter.

Blick said not all dying patients will want the ability to take their own life, but he said they should be given the choice.

"This is not for everybody. We do realize there are people that do not believe in this for religious beliefs, and I respect that. There are no issues over that," he said. "But there are those subsets of people that do not want to go through the suffering that they have to go through."

Cathy Ludlum, of Manchester, a disabled-rights activist who has spinal muscular atrophy, said she is concerned the Public Health Committee has decided to hold the public hearing and worries the issue of doctor-assisted suicide will not go away soon.

"Until people are really educated about the issues, it's going to keep coming up, even if it's defeated this time," she said, adding how she wants lawmakers to focus more on "giving people a good life than giving people a good death."

8

The Death with Dignity Movement Endangers People with Disabilities

Diane Coleman

Diane Coleman is founder and president of Not Dead Yet, a national organization advocating against assisted suicide, headquartered in Forest Park, Illinois.

Disability rights groups, such as Not Dead Yet, oppose the Death with Dignity movement because they believe it devalues the lives of disabled people and makes them even more vulnerable than they already are, both in society and in the health-care system. Economic pressures are a strong incentive for medical providers to offer the death option, as people with chronic illnesses and disabilities are often consumers of expensive medical care during their lifetimes. Offering to pay for death assistance based on the fact that someone is disabled or ill is actually discrimination under the Americans with Disabilities Act. Assisted suicide and euthanasia are lethal forms of discrimination, and they endanger the lives of people with disabilities.

"*I* don't want to live like this one more day," she said firmly. "I've had enough." She had been forced, at 26, to leave her masters program. Her car had been repossessed. Following a miscarriage, her marriage had broken up. Her brother had drowned. And now her mother had been diagnosed with cancer.

One night, she turned up in a hospital, moaning that she just wanted to die. She was a competent adult, and her reasons for living were gone, so the hospital should not interfere. In fact, the doctor should cooperate, so she would not have to worry about botching her suicide and making things worse. She had lost more than most could bear. She just wanted the suffering to end. So she called a lawyer to sue the hospital to help her end it all.

Let us say that this is a hypothetical. If it were a question on a law school essay test, what would the issues be? What laws would apply? Would she win or lose? Lose, right?

But it is not a hypothetical. It is a real case. Elizabeth Bouvia "won" the right to starve herself in a hospital while receiving morphine and comfort care. What facts are missing from the synopsis above? Well, chief among them was that she was born with cerebral palsy, and she used a wheelchair to get around.

In the critical period after [a disabling] injury, many people who now enjoy their lives report that they could easily have been swayed to "choose" death.

Not Dead Yet

The case galvanized the disability community in southern California from 1983 to 1985. Members provided everything from expert testimony to street protests, calling attention to something that was obvious to people with disabilities and completely foreign to everyone else: Ms. Bouvia wanted to die, not because of her disability, but because of social losses that could move anyone to despair. Community members also wanted to question—and change—the assumption that, in a case like Ms. Bouvia's, the simple fact of disability changes everything.

Not Dead Yet is a national disability rights group that opposes the legalization of assisted suicide and euthanasia. Many of our allies in the civil rights and health care movements have found this hard to understand. Isn't this about individual autonomy and rights, they ask? No, we say, it's about disability discrimination, a profit-oriented health care system, and a legal system that does not guarantee the equal protection of the law.

Disability Discrimination

In 1989, the U.S. Civil Rights Commission issued a 153-page report entitled "Medical Discrimination Against Children with Disabilities." Among the events considered by the Commission was an experiment conducted from 1977 to 1982 at the Children's Hospital of Oklahoma. Doctors there developed a "quality of life" formula for babies with spina bifida, taking into account the socioeconomic status of the baby's family to determine what to advise families about a simple but life-and-death procedure. Better-off families were provided a realistic and optimistic picture of their child's potential. Poor families were provided a pessimistic picture. All of the families who were given an optimistic picture asked for medical care for their children. Conversely, four out of five poor families agreed not to treat their children, and twenty-four babies died. The U.S. Civil Rights Commission concluded:

> To accept a projected negative quality of life ... based on the difficulties society will cause ... rather than tackling the difficulties themselves, is unacceptable. The Commission rejects the view that an acceptable answer to discrimination and prejudice is to assure the "right to die" to those against whom the discrimination and prejudice exists.

Parents' early beliefs about what their disabled children's lives can or will be like are very much shaped by health care providers. But the majority of people with disabilities acquire their disabilities some time after birth. Their beliefs about what life with a disability is like are shaped by a society that devalues people with disabilities. Then, when they become disabled, their beliefs about what their own lives with disabilities will be like are shaped by health care providers. So the story remains the same. Newly injured people may be particularly at risk. Eight thousand people injure their spinal cords each year, and 99,000 are hospitalized with moderate to severe head injuries. In the critical period after injury, many people who now enjoy their lives report that they could easily have been swayed to "choose" death.

A Double Standard for Suicide Intervention

Society has established ways of responding to someone who expresses a desire to die. If you see someone on a ledge, you do not yell "Jump!" and you certainly do not push. In theory, suicide intervention involves asking why and trying to address the factors leading to despair. Many professionals have legal duties in this regard. But now we hear proposals to carve out an exception for people with disabilities, generally people with expensive disabilities, old or young, terminal or even just "incurable." A bill being considered in New Hampshire, for example, defines a "terminal illness" as any incurable condition that shortens one's overall life span, and the Hemlock Society's website defines it merely as an incurable one.

Under the Americans with Disabilities Act (ADA), a disability is defined in part as a "physical or mental impairment that substantially limits one or more of the major life activities of [the] individual," such as seeing, hearing, learning, working, and self-care. It is also well established that the ADA covers persons with cancer or HIV. People with terminal illnesses generally qualify as people with disabilities. Moreover, health care providers are subject to the nondiscrimination provisions of the ADA. What has not been considered by most civil rights defenders is that any double standard for suicide intervention that is based on whether a person does or does not have a disability violates the ADA. That includes the assisted suicide law that went into effect in Oregon over a year ago.

The Economics of Health Care

Today, adding economic pressures to the medical discrimination that existed at the time of the Civil Rights Commission report, Medicare and Medicaid are facing major budget crises. Medicare already does not pay for prescription medications. Since 1998, the nation's top health maintenance organizations have been pulling out of state Medicaid programs that serve poor, elderly, and disabled people. Federal courts have been upholding the rights of private health insurance companies to cap HIV/AIDS benefits at $25,000 in policies that cap other benefits at $1 million. This threatens to force individuals with AIDS into the weakening publicly funded system. There is apparently no legal reason that such caps could not contractually be placed on other expensive conditions as well.

Offering a right to die as the only alternative to a nursing home cannot be considered a victory for liberty.

Of course, disability is not the only basis of health care discrimination. Poverty and race are well-documented factors in access to health care. On June 17, 1998, the *Journal of the American Medical Association* reported that people of color are significantly less likely to receive pain medication than whites, even aspirin. This study involved over 13,000 cancer patients and confirmed the racial differences found in previous studies. Recent reports show that the number of the uninsured in the United States is now at 44 million and continues to rise.

The Oregon assisted suicide law is now offered as a "model" approach to legalization. But how does this "carefully crafted" statute, supposedly filled with safeguards, address the harsh realities of today's profit-driven health care system, a system that offers few choices to the people whose need for services is a drain on the bottom line?

Perhaps most relevant is the informed consent provision. Everyone who receives assisted suicide must first be informed of "the feasible alternatives, including, but not limited to, comfort care, hospice care, and pain control" (Section 3.01(2)(e)). These feasible alternatives are not defined in the lengthy definitions section of the law. Nor does the law require that any desired alternatives, feasible or otherwise, be paid for. The law does not even provide for payment as a "last resort," only when all other payment options prove unavailable.

Unfriendly Courts

The civil courts have already established numerous precedents for treating people with significant but nonterminal disabilities in the same way that terminally ill people are treated. The Bouvia case mentioned previously was followed by a line of several cases the disability community now refers to as the "give me liberty or give me death" cases. In them, people with quadriplegia who use ventilators—people like Christopher Reeve—asked not to be forced to live in nursing homes for lack of home health services, but that liberty interest was ignored. They subsequently gave up and asked for assisted death. The media had no qualms publicizing that as a crusade for liberty, and the courts expanded the right to refuse treatment, resulting in many deaths. Offering a right to die as the only alternative to a nursing home cannot be considered a victory for liberty.

The criminal court system has not provided equal protection for people with disabilities, either. Jack Kevorkian claimed 130 victims, most of them not terminally ill, and all killed well outside the parameters of any proposed assisted suicide bill. Nonetheless, he was only prosecuted for seven deaths, and only convicted of one. In addition, studies of sentencing patterns when parents kill their disabled children show a disturbing lack of parity to sentences imposed when parents kill nondisabled children. From prosecutorial discretion to conviction and sentencing disparities, people with disabilities do not see much evidence that the courts treat their lives as being as valuable as their nondisabled counterparts'.

Significant evidence exists that neither the civil nor the criminal court systems will enforce the "safeguards" in the Oregon law. The law's culpability standard is the lowest possible, mere "good faith" compliance. There are no investigatory provisions, and the statute does more to secure every form of legal immunity for all participants in assisted suicide than it does to secure individual rights. "Safeguard" problems that have already been reported in the press—involving depression, active euthanasia, family coercion, and lack of informed consent—have passed with little comment.

Discrimination against any minority, including people with disabilities, should not be put up to majority vote.

Since the Oregon law immunizes all participants in an assisted suicide, to what extent might it be interpreted by the public as permission to pressure or even hasten the deaths of family members without the involvement of health care providers? According to a study by the National Center on Elder Abuse, 450,000 seniors were abused or neglected in 1996. Among known perpetrators, 90 percent were family members, and two-thirds of those involved the spouse or an adult child. The Federal Bureau of Investigation reports that 55.9 percent of all homicides of children up to age eleven are committed by family members, as are 21.2 percent of homicides of persons over age fifty. Yet these significant indicators of risk have been ignored by assisted suicide proponents or treated as irrelevant.

Unfriendly Courts

In March 1997, a leading bioethics journal, *The Hastings Center Report*, published a cover article entitled "Is There a Duty to Die?" The article led off with favorable comments on former Colorado Governor Richard Lamm's claim that the elderly have a duty to die.

On December 3, 1997, the [right-to-die advocacy group] Hemlock Society issued a widely ignored press release in which its Executive Director, Faye Girsh, called for laws allowing family members and other "agents" to procure court orders to kill "a demented parent, a suffering severely disable [sic] spouse, or a child" if their lives are "too burdensome to continue."

More recently, Professor Peter Singer has been recruited into a tenured and endowed chair in bioethics at Princeton University. Singer works to popularize a utilitarian ethic holding that it is moral to kill newborns with even minor health impairments and that older children and adults with significant cognitive disabilities can also be morally killed. His theories provide a theoretical foundation for nonvoluntary euthanasia, partly as a means of rationing health care. What is often overlooked is that Princeton University's president chairs the National Bioethics Advisory Commission appointed by the U.S. president.

A Life or Death Matter

Discrimination against any minority, including people with disabilities, should not be put up to majority vote. The Supreme Court found that federal law trumped states rights on discrimination in 1954. Assisted suicide and euthanasia are lethal forms of discrimination, and the Supreme Court should decide against state sovereignty once again.

Assisted suicide has been marketed to the American public as a step toward increasing individual freedom, but choice is an empty slogan in a world full of pressures on people with chronic illnesses and disabilities. Now is not the time to establish a public policy securing the profits of a health care system that abandons those most in need and would bury the evidence of their crime.

9

Choosing to Die Can Be a Rational Decision for the Elderly

Julia Medew

Julia Medew is the health editor at the Australian newspaper The Age.

The story of Beverley Broadbent, an eighty-three-year-old Australian woman who chose to end her life despite not being terminally ill, reflects the mindset of many elderly people who would prefer a peaceful, dignified death at a time of their own choosing to years of physical deterioration and functional decline in a nursing home. Before her death, Broadbent explained her decision to the media and made the case that she was making an entirely rational choice of her own volition. Critics, meanwhile, maintain that allowing elderly people to legally end their lives would create a "culture of death" and eventually lead to allowing the same thing for vulnerable individuals, such as disabled children or those with dementia.

Beverley Broadbent was not dying of a terminal illness, nor was she depressed or unhappy. But at 83, she wanted to die.

After living a rich and satisfying life, the [Australian] woman said the ageing process had come to feel like a disease that was robbing her of her physical and mental fitness. In February [2013], she said she had had enough.

"I look well and I walk well so people think I'm fine. But I have so many things wrong with me," she said. "The balance is gone. It's taking so much time for me to keep fit to enjoy myself that there's not enough time to enjoy myself."

In several interviews with Fairfax Media, Ms Broadbent said she planned to take her own life so she could have a peaceful, dignified death. She said she did not want her health to deteriorate to the point where she had dementia or found herself in a nursing home with no way out.

The environmental activist chose to tell her story because she believed many elderly people wanted to die when they felt their life was complete, but lacked the means to go gently.

"I can't understand why people who really want to can't have the means to go with the help of a doctor in a dignified manner at the time that they choose," she said.

"They are not asking anybody else to do it, they don't want to pressure anyone else to do it, they just want to have the right to do what I'm doing. I hope people can see how sensible it is and that I'm not stupid, I'm not depressed, I'm not sad. I'm having a good life that I'm enjoying right to the last minute."

In recent years, [Australia] has seen an increasing number of cases in which people have made apparently rational decisions to end their lives because they were suffering a chronic or terminal illness.

The "Peaceful Pill"

Ms Broadbent said she had acquired some barbiturates—the drugs euthanasia advocates call the "peaceful pill"—and planned to take them when the time was right.

She died at home in her bed on February 11 [2013].

When she explained her choice, Ms Broadbent said her fear of deteriorating to the point where she would be unable to end her life made her want to go sooner rather than later. She said if physician-assisted suicide was legal, she might have pushed on knowing she could end her life at any time.

"I can't wait, I can't take the risk," she said.

Her story comes as the Coroners Court of Victoria launches an investigation into suicide to establish how common it is and what factors are driving it. In recent years, the court has seen an increasing number of cases in which people have made apparently rational decisions to end their lives because they were suffering a chronic or terminal illness.

Euthanasia campaigner Rodney Syme, who met Ms Broadbent several times before her death, said he believed she had not been depressed and had made a choice that many other elderly people would like to emulate.

He said an increasing number of older people were contacting him on the issue. Many wanted to avoid nursing homes.

Although polls show about 80 percent of Australians support voluntary euthanasia for people with a terminal illness, Dr Syme said the question of elderly people being given the right to die had not been publicly debated in Australia.

This was despite the fact that many elderly people were severely disabled and experiencing great suffering on a par with that caused by cancer or other painful diseases, he said.

"Unfortunately, often people in Bev's situation who do try to talk about these things are patronised by their family, who say: 'Don't talk like that gran, no, no, no, you're all right.' They are put down and patronised, no one gives them a voice," he said.

"I think it's an issue for which a lot of people probably have very quiet and hidden opinions. It's an issue which is going to assume greater and greater importance and it's about time the community started to debate it in a logical way."

Public Attitudes Have Influence

But Dr Katrina Haller, senior executive officer of Right to Life Australia, said Ms Broadbent's story exacerbated her concern that elderly people were increasingly being viewed as a burden when they should be valued, supported and not "dumped in old people's homes."

She said increasing discussion about elderly people taking up too many hospital beds, for example, could be encouraging suicide when the community was spending a large amount of money trying to prevent people taking their own lives.

"Elderly people can be coerced into feeling they are a burden on their family and their friends and the medical staff at hospital—and hospitals have other agendas, don't they? They want to free up beds and minimise the money spent on people," she said.

A Culture of Death

Dr Haller said that although Ms Broadbent's story was an emotional one and might be hard to argue with, it did not amount to a case for legalising physician-assisted suicide, which would create a culture of death and turn doctors into killers.

She said legislating a right for elderly people to die would inevitably start a debate about others, including people with dementia and children with disabilities.

"Where do you draw the line? ... In Belgium and the Netherlands [where euthanasia is legal for some people] the door gets opened a bit wider as years go by," she said.

10

Vulnerable People Can Be Coerced into Choosing Death

Wesley Smith

Wesley Smith is a lawyer and the associate director of the International Task Force on Euthanasia and Assisted Suicide.

People often point to Oregon's Death with Dignity law as a model piece of right-to-die legislation, but it is not. The law is misguided, and in some cases it will even pay for a patient's assisted suicide but not for medical treatment that might prolong his or her life. Advocates insist the Oregon law is proof that assisted suicide can be done without abuses, but for many of the most vulnerable people—the poor, elderly, and disabled—the right to die can very easily become a duty to die. People often choose assisted suicide because they are afraid of becoming a burden on the state or their families, and that fear is validated not only by society's attitudes but by the availability of legal assisted suicide in the first place.

Imagine that you have lung cancer. It has been in remission, but tests show the cancer has returned and is likely to be terminal. Still, there is some hope. Chemotherapy could extend your life, if not save it. You ask to begin treatment. But you soon receive more devastating news. A letter from the government informs you that the cost of chemotherapy is deemed an unjustified expense for the limited extra time it

Wesley Smith, "'Right to Die' Can Become a 'Duty to Die'—Vulnerable People Can Be Bullied into Assisted Suicide," *The Telegraph*, February 20, 2009. Copyright © Telegraph Media Group Limited 2009. All rights reserved. Reproduced by permission.

would provide. However, the government is not without compassion. You are informed that whenever you are ready, it will gladly pay for your assisted suicide.

Think that's an alarmist scenario to scare you away from supporting "death with dignity"? Wrong. That is exactly what happened last year to two cancer patients in Oregon, where assisted suicide is legal.

Barbara Wagner had recurrent lung cancer and Randy Stroup had prostate cancer. Both were on Medicaid, the state's health insurance plan for the poor that . . . is rationed. The state denied both treatment, but told them it would pay for their assisted suicide. "It dropped my chin to the floor," Stroup told the media. "[How could they] not pay for medication that would help my life, and yet offer to pay to end my life?" (Wagner eventually received free medication from the drug manufacturer. She has since died. The denial of chemotherapy to Stroup was reversed on appeal after his story hit the media.)

Oregon Law Is No Ideal Model

Despite Wagner and Stroup's cases, advocates continue to insist that Oregon proves assisted suicide can be legalised with no abuses. But the more one learns about the actual experience, the shakier such assurances become.

At a meeting in the House of Commons on Monday night [February 16, 2009] hosted by the anti-euthanasia charity Alert and Labour MP [Member of Parliament] Brian Iddon, I hope to bring home to MPs and the British public just how dangerous it would be to legalise euthanasia. The Oregon experiment shows how easily the "right to die" can become a "duty to die" for vulnerable and depressed people fearful of becoming a burden on the state or their relatives. I know that a powerful and emotive campaign is being waged in the UK media—using heart-rending cases such as multiple sclerosis sufferer Debbie Purdy—to inveigle Parliament into changing the law.

Miss Purdy, who lost in the Appeal Court on Thursday, wants to secure a legal guarantee that her husband would not be prosecuted if he accompanied her to the Dignitas clinic in Switzerland—one of the few places where euthanasia is legal. Much as I sympathise with her plight, such a guarantee would lure us on to the slippery slope where the old and the sick come under pressure to end their lives.

When a scared and depressed patient asks for poison pills and their doctor's response is to pull out the lethal prescription pad, it confirms the patient's worst fears—that they are a burden, that they are less worth loving.

A study published in the *Journal of Internal Medicine* last year, for example, found that doctors in Oregon write lethal prescriptions for patients who are not experiencing significant symptoms and that assisted suicide practice has had little do with any inability to alleviate pain—the fear of which is a chief selling point for legalisation.

Decisions Based on Fear, Not Facts

The report said that family members described loved ones who pursue "physician-assisted death" as individuals for whom being in control is important, who anticipate the negative aspects of dying and who believe the impending loss of self and quality of life will be intolerable. They fear becoming a burden to others, yet want to die at home. Concerns about what may be experienced in the future were substantially more powerful reasons than what they experienced at that point in time.

When a scared and depressed patient asks for poison pills and their doctor's response is to pull out the lethal prescription pad, it confirms the patient's worst fears—that they are a burden, that they are less worth loving. Hospices are geared to address such concerns. But effective hospice care is undermined when a badly needed mental health intervention is easily avoided via a state-sanctioned, physician-prescribed overdose of lethal pills.

Do the guidelines protect depressed people in Oregon? Hardly. The law does not require treatment when depression is suspected, and very few terminal patients who ask for assisted suicide are referred for psychiatric consultations. In 2008, not one patient who received a lethal prescription was referred by the prescribing doctor for a mental health evaluation.

No Due Diligence

As palliative care physician Dr Kathleen Foley and psychiatrist Herbert Hendin, an expert on suicide prevention, wrote in a scathing exposé of Oregon assisted suicide, physicians are able to "assist in suicide without inquiring into the source of the medical, psychological, social and existential concerns that usually underlie requests . . . even though this type of inquiring produces the kind of discussion that often leads to relief for patients and makes assisted suicide seem unnecessary."

Oregon has become the model for how assisted suicide is supposed to work. But for those who dig beneath the sloganeering and feel-good propaganda, it becomes clear that legalising assisted suicide leads to abandonment, bad medical practice and a disregard for the importance of patients' lives.

11

Physician-Assisted Suicide Laws Are Actually Seldom Used

Serena Gordon

Serena Gordon is a journalist who has written for HealthDay, a consumer health news service, since 1999.

Washington State enacted a Death with Dignity law in March 2009. Since that time, a relatively small number of people have taken advantage of life-ending prescriptions, suggesting that critics' fears about the program are misplaced. In three years, just 255 people have received prescriptions to hasten their deaths, although far fewer actually used them to do so. Every year, more than fifty thousand people die in Washington, so the number of people using the Death with Dignity program is actually "miniscule." Supporters of the law say that these statistics should alleviate concerns that the program would cause a spike in suicide among terminally ill people.

Physician-assisted suicide laws can raise controversy and concern with their passage, but a new study from Washington State suggests many of those fears may be unfounded.

Washington's Death With Dignity Act hasn't lead to scores of terminally ill people seeking lethal prescriptions, the researchers report: Almost three years after the law was enacted, just 255 people had obtained a lethal prescription from a physician.

Of those 255 prescriptions, 40 were written for terminal cancer patients at the Seattle Cancer Care Alliance. And, in the new study, doctors there found that only 60 percent (24 people) of their patients chose to use their prescription to hasten their death.

"Most Americans say that they want to die at home with family members around, not in pain and with their mental faculties as in tact as possible. But, not everyone is achieving that kind of good death. For the rare number of people using the Death With Dignity program, we are reassured by the high numbers of people who use palliative or hospice care and who talk with their families about this decision," said study author Dr. Elizabeth Trice Loggers, medical director of palliative care at the Seattle Cancer Care Alliance.

Results of the study appear in the April 11 [2013] issue of the *New England Journal of Medicine.*

Physician-assisted death, also known as physician-assisted suicide, is currently legal in Oregon, Washington and Montana. Other states, among them Hawaii, Pennsylvania and Vermont, are considering legislation to allow physician-assisted deaths for people with terminal illnesses.

Putting Safeguards in Place

Washington's law was passed in November 2008, and enacted in March 2009. The Death With Dignity Act contains a number of safeguards. The illness must be terminal, and the patient must be competent. The request must be voluntary, the person making the request can't have a mental illness that might impair their judgment and they must understand what treatment and palliative care options are available.

Additional safeguards have been put in place at the Seattle Cancer Care Alliance that include no advertising of the program, no new patients whose sole purpose is to access the Death With Dignity program and voluntary participation by physicians and other staff members.

From March 2009 through December 2011, 114 patients at Seattle Cancer Care Alliance asked about the Death With Dignity program. Of these, 44 chose not to pursue the program at all.

> *The most common reasons people cited for participating in the program were loss of autonomy, an inability to engage in enjoyable activities and a loss of dignity.*

Another 30 people initiated the process, but either chose not to continue to the next step, or died in the interim.

Participation Numbers

Forty patients received a prescription for a lethal dose of secobarbital, a powerful sedative. Twenty-four patients died after ingesting the medication. On average, the time from ingestion to death was 35 minutes. The remaining 16 patients chose not to use their prescription and eventually died from their cancer.

Those who participated were mostly married white males with more than a high school education. Their ages ranged from 42 to 91, according to the study authors. All had been diagnosed with terminal cancer.

The most common reasons people cited for participating in the program were loss of autonomy, an inability to engage in enjoyable activities and a loss of dignity.

"Each year, there are over 50,000 deaths in Washington State, and cancer is the second leading cause of death. The number who chose to participate in the Death With Dignity program is miniscule. This study shows that people are not making these decisions lightly," Trice Loggers said. She added that patients and their families have expressed gratitude for the program.

Dr. Gary Kennedy, director of geriatric psychiatry at Montefiore Medical Center in New York City, said he thought the

Seattle Cancer Care Alliance took great care to be as neutral as they could, so that it was up to the patients to pursue physician-assisted death.

"Before these laws were enacted, one of the concerns in the suicide prevention community was that these laws would be promoted," Kennedy said. And, while he was pleased to see that there was no such promotion, he still has concerns about physician-assisted death programs.

A Look at Demographics

He noted that most of the people who participated in the program were older, white males. As a group, older, white males tend to have higher than normal suicide rates, even without a terminal diagnosis, according to Kennedy.

While one of the requirements of the law is that someone must be competent and free of mental illness that could impair their judgment, Kennedy said it can be difficult to diagnose depression in terminally ill patients. It wasn't clear from the study if people only met with social workers, or if they were referred to psychologists or psychiatrists, according to Kennedy.

The good news, he said, is that "this law has not led to a whole rush to suicide in the terminally ill."

Trice Loggers reiterated: "Our job is to cure cancer. But, there are situations where we just can't do that. Among those who opted for Death With Dignity, the number using hospice was 80 percent or greater. They were able to include their family and to die at home, which is consistent with how most people say they want to die."

"It's important to remember that in Washington, this law was passed by referendum. Approximately 60 percent of voters said this was an appropriate end-of-life decision," she noted.

12

The Right to Die
Is Not a Civil Right

Ira Byock

Ira Byock, MD, is a palliative care physician and author of The
Best Care Possible: A Physician's Quest to Transform Care
Through the End of Life. *More information is available at*
TheBestCarePossible.org.

When viewed as an issue of human rights, physician-assisted
suicide is a very attractive concept to liberals, but there is actu-
ally no civil right to commit suicide. If the political left would
look deeper into the issue, they would see that "the right to die,"
"death with dignity," and "self-deliverance" are nothing more
than empty slogans meant to reshape moral thought. Nothing in
Death with Dignity laws protects sick individuals from the eco-
nomic incentives to die that are built into today's profit-driven
system of medical care. Instead of legalizing assisted suicide, the
left should focus on fixing American's broken health-care system,
improving training for physicians, and ensuring high quality
end-of-life care.

Editor's Note: The 2012 Death with Dignity Act ballot proposal
in Massachusetts failed to pass by a slim margin: 49 percent yes
to 51 percent no.

The issue of legalizing physician-assisted suicide doesn't fall
cleanly along liberal-conservative lines. However, it's fair
to say that most social conservatives ardently oppose assisted
suicide, while a clear majority on the political left support le-

galization. That's the case in Massachusetts where Question 2 is on November's [2012] ballot, and according to recent polling is very likely to pass.

I am an outlier, in that I am a registered Democrat and progressive, as well as a physician who has cared for people with life-threatening conditions for more than three decades. I support universal health care, voting rights, disability rights, women's rights, Planned Parenthood, gay marriage, alternative energy, and gun control. I yearn to see an end to the war on drugs and the war in Afghanistan. And, I am convinced that legalization of physician-assisted suicide is something my fellow progressives should fear and loathe.

Suicide Slogans

When cast as a rights issue, it's hard for progressives to resist. But "the right to die" is just a slogan. No civil right to commit suicide exists in any social compact. Human beings have a biologically imposed *obligation* to die; and, as [French philosopher] Jean Paul Sartre reminded us, suicide is always an option. However, even if a civic right to suicide did exist, *suicide* and *assisted suicide* are very different things. Suicide might be a purely private act; but *physician-assisted suicide* involves two people, one of whom is trained, certified, licensed, and compensated by society.

> *In actuality, criteria for physician-assisted suicide in Oregon are more liberal than eligibility for hospice care.*

Supporters of initiatives to legalize physician-assisted suicide worry about people who die badly. On that we agree. If the moral worth of a society can be measured by how well it cares for the most vulnerable of its members, the America in which I live and practice medicine scores poorly. Much of the suffering I see among people with advanced illness is preventable. Many of the indignities I witness are imposed.

Assisted Suicide Won't Fix Medical System

Sick people commonly endure undertreated physical suffering and a dizzying array of system-based personal assaults. There is a maze of appointments, irrational insurance hoops and requirements, and indecipherable bills. I hear patients express embarrassment at becoming a burden to those they love, dread at the prospect of draining their family's savings and shame of being forced into medical bankruptcy. Public policies could go a long way to dissolving this quagmire, but legalizing physician-assisted suicide isn't one of them. Giving doctors lethal authority would address none of the deficiencies in medical practice, health care financing or social services that bring ill people to contemplate ending their lives.

Oregon is often held up as an example of a place where legalized physician-assisted suicide has worked well. Its Death with Dignity Act is a template for legislation in other states, including Massachusetts. It is widely assumed that if a terminally ill individual qualifies for a lethal prescription, he or she automatically qualifies for hospice care. Not true. In actuality, criteria for physician-assisted suicide in Oregon are more liberal (sic) than eligibility for hospice care.

Under scrutiny from the federal government in its zeal to curtail Medicare fraud and abuse, hospice programs are under pressure to discharge patients who are not actively declining. In 2010, 16% of hospice patients in America were eventually discharged from hospice care. These are people with cancer, emphysema, heart failure, or dementia whose conditions improve slightly, often as a result of the meticulous care hospice has been providing. They are still dying, just not quickly enough for the bureaucracy.

Role Reversal

No provision in Oregon's Death with Dignity Act, nor in the proposed Massachusetts law protects patients who obtain lethal prescriptions from losing hospice services if they live a bit too long.

Proponents of physician-assisted suicide portray the American Medical Association's and Massachusetts' Medical Association's steadfast opposition as self-serving. But this turns the situation on its head. In this instance the medical associations are advancing progressive values. Since antiquity, doctors have had more power than patients. From the earliest times the profession has honored self-imposed boundaries put in place to protect vulnerable people. Clinical Ethics 101 includes three inviolable prohibitions: Doctors must not intentionally kill a patient, must not have sex with a patient, and must not financially benefit beyond reasonable compensation for their professional services.

An authentic progressive agenda for improving the way we die would begin by tying physician and hospital payments to quality of care, not quantity of tests and treatments, and doubling the ratio of nurses and aides to residents in nursing homes.

In 2008 Barbara Wagner sought chemotherapy for late stage lung cancer. The Oregon Health Plan office refused to authorize the $4,000 per month treatment because it was not approved for her condition, but listed among the services it would pay for were prescription drugs to end her life. "To say to someone, we'll pay for you to die, but not for you to live; it's cruel," Wagner told the *Eugene Register-Guard* [newspaper].

Orwellian Overtones

The term Orwellian is overused, but seems apt here. [English novelist and journalist George] Orwell understood the power of language to reshape moral thought. In today's "Newspeak" the [assisted-suicide advocacy group] Hemlock Society morphed into Compassion and Choices, which promotes "death with dignity" and objects to the word "suicide," preferring "aid-in-dying" and "self-deliverance." These terms sound more wholesome, but the undisguised act is a morally primitive, socially regressive, response to basic human needs. Progressives in Massachusetts who vote for Question 2 should remember that by the end of Orwell's *1984* the protagonist, Winston Smith, loved [totalitarian dictator] Big Brother.

An authentic progressive agenda for improving the way we die would begin by tying physician and hospital payments to quality of care, not quantity of tests and treatments, and doubling the ratio of nurses and aides to residents in nursing homes. (Honoring the inherent dignity of a person starts with ensuring there's someone to answer the bell when the person needs help getting to the bathroom.) Also high on a liberal agenda should be repealing regulations that require sick people to give up life-prolonging treatments to receive hospice care. Finally, it's past time to insist that every medical student receives adequate training and passes competency tests in symptom management, communication and counseling related to serious illness and dying—skills that most physicians lack today.

America is failing people who are facing the end of life and those who love and care for them. Giving licensed physicians the authority to write lethal prescriptions is not a progressive thing to do.

13

Right-to-Die Laws Could Extend to Healthy People

Jacob M. Appel

Bioethicist and medical historian Jacob M. Appel writes about the confluence of law, medicine, and philosophy. His work has appeared in The New York Times, Chicago Tribune, Journal of Medical Ethics, *and the* Hastings Center Report, *among other publications.*

Existing Death with Dignity laws specify that only people with six months or less to live may have access to life-ending medicines. There is a push within the right-to-die movement to extend that eligibility to mentally competent individuals who live with intractable pain and extreme disabilities that make it impossible for them to end their own lives. This presents a complex moral dilemma, but an even bigger quandary is whether healthy individuals should be permitted the same option to end their lives. Personal autonomy is the cornerstone of both medical ethics and American democracy. One's life is one's own and no one else's, so individuals should have the right to self-determination concerning their deaths. Suicide on demand for everyone is worthy of open discussion and serious consideration.

Advocates for physician-assisted suicide have in recent years focused upon the rights of the terminally ill and severely disabled to control their own destinies. Oregon's Death With Dignity Act of 1994 and Washington's Initiative 1000 of 2008 both limit medical providers to prescribing life-ending drugs to situations in which patients have only six months remaining to live. Many advocates for a "right to die" would also like to see such opportunities expanded to include fully-competent patients with locked-in syndromes, quadriplegias, and other forms of extreme disability, specifically in cases where these victims express an ongoing and rational desire to die, but are physically incapable of ending their own lives. To deny such patients assistance is, to my own thinking, a form of torture by inaction. However, the physician-assisted suicide movement—and western society generally—must now confront a far more challenging ethical dilemma: How should we handle healthy individuals who request medical assistance to end their own lives?

Despite the cries of alarmists, no sane people intend to force assisted suicide upon the unwilling to fulfill some dystopic vision.

This week [July 2009] the simultaneous suicides of British conductor Edward Downes and his wife, Joan, in Switzerland, have generated considerable controversy. While seventy-four year-old Joan apparently suffered from an imminently fatal cancer, her eighty-five year-old husband was "merely" increasingly deaf and blind. To critics interested in drawing bright and arbitrary lines, she might have qualified as a terminal case, while he might not have. However, most compassionate individuals, once they embrace the legitimacy of assisted suicide under some circumstances, would have little difficulty permitting these brave souls to die together. But what if one partner had been dying while the other had been in the full bloom of health? This is no longer an abstract philosophical inquiry. For George and Betty Coumbias of Vancouver [British Columbia, Canada], it has become a pressing matter of life and love and death.

The Coumbias Case

As reported in the media, George Coumbias suffers from debilitating and potentially-deadly cardiac disease. His wife, Betty, also in her early seventies, is in good health. However, according to human rights attorney Ludwig Minelli, the director of the Swiss suicide-assistance organization, Dignitas, Mrs. Coumbias wishes to die alongside her husband during simultaneous suicides. She explained her motives in a 2007 documentary film, *The Suicide Tourist*: "From the day we got married, [my husband] was all my life. . . . I love my two daughters, but I love him more, and I don't think I can face life without him, and since we read about Dignitas, we felt, what would be better than to die together, you know, to die in each other's arms?" The Coumbias are not the first couple to express a desire to depart side-by-side. In one highly-publicized case, on New Year's Day 2002, the octogenarian son and daughter-in-law of Admiral Chester Nimitz carried out a carefully-orchestrated death pact—even writing checks to their children dated January 2 in order to avoid taxes. Other couples have done the same, although outside the media spotlight. But the Coumbias may be the first pair to seek legal sanction for such an arrangement. Minelli intends to petition the Canton [administrative division] of Zurich [Switzerland], where assisted-suicide is already permitted for the unwell, to grant local physicians the authority to prescribe lethal medication to healthy people. If his request is rejected, he plans to appeal to the Administrative Court of Zurich and even to the Federal Court of Switzerland. How unfortunate that so much cross-border legal wrangling is necessary for the Coumbias to do as they wish with their own bodies.

Autonomy and Alarmism

I do not know whether Betty Coumbias' decision to end her own life reflects deep wisdom or poor judgment—much as I do not know whether she will enjoy an afterlife of eternal harmony or experience a sudden and irreversible cessation of being. Personally, I happen to find her devotion to her ill husband admirably romantic and all-too-rare. Yet this is beside the point. What matters is that the person best suited to determine Betty Coumbias' destiny is Betty Coumbias. Personal autonomy has long served as the core principal of both American medical ethics and liberal democracy. Individual choice should not yield to societal preference simply because the question is no longer how to live, but how to die.

I do not mean to suggest that autonomy does not have its appropriate limits or that suicide-on-demand should not be subject to meaningful regulation. Mental capacity—the legal standard for making medical decisions—should be required to honor such a request. Psychotic patients, for example, ought not be allowed to kill themselves during psychosis. Similarly, a seventeen-year-old girl, distraught after an argument with her boyfriend, should not be able to walk into a hospital emergency room and demand an immediate overdose of Tylenol. Society is within its bounds to require rational, informed choices, expressed over a reasonable period of time. Efforts should be made to ascertain that no undue pressure or duress lies behind the longing to die. Indian widows, coerced into throwing themselves onto funeral pyres, do not further the cause of individual liberty. Needless to say, despite the cries of alarmists, no sane people intend to force assisted suicide upon the unwilling to fullfill some dystopic vision.

Suicide for the Healthy

If the healthy are granted the right to die, gray areas will inevitably arise. That does not mean that all areas are gray. A standard that one might use in determining whether to approve a suicide request could be: Under these circumstances, would *any* reasonable person make such a request? In the case of Betty and George Coumbias, the answer is an easy yes. A consistent plea to die in the arms of a beloved spouse, expressed over a period of two years, is not a wish that a set of officious Platonic [unchanging] guardians should second-guess. If Betty Coumbias had only six months left to live and expressed such a desire, most assisted-suicide advocates would support her cause. Why should she have any less control over her own life because she is fortunate enough to be in good health?

Some supporters of physician-assisted suicide may worry that assisted suicide for the healthy is too much, too soon, and risks turning the general public against a noble cause. That is not a concern to be dismissed lightly. But Betty Coumbias does not owe her body to the assisted-suicide movement any more than she owes it to those who oppose assisted suicide. Her life is hers and hers alone. A free society, to be truly worthy of that name, owes her, and other healthy, competent individuals with similar wishes, the right to live and to end their lives on their own terms.

14

Legal Euthanasia for Sick Babies Does Not Increase the Practice

Jo Carlowe

Freelance journalist Jo Carlowe writes features and news for national newspapers, consumer magazines, websites, and professional journals.

Many people fear that legalizing euthanasia for babies who are hopelessly sick would lead to an increase in the practice. Such euthanasia is legal in The Netherlands, following a very strict set of rules called the Groningen Protocol, which was enacted in 2005. Researchers examining the use of the protocol discovered that active euthanasia is rarely performed and that most eligible cases (95 percent) instead end via infanticide, in which medical treatment or food and water is simply withheld from a terminally ill infant rather than euthanasia being actively performed. The researchers note that the euthanasia numbers may be so low because advanced prenatal screening procedures that detect severe abnormalities give parents the opportunity to terminate the pregnancy.

Fears that legalising euthanasia for very sick newborns would prompt the start of a "slippery slope" are groundless.

These are the findings from experts who architected a dedicated protocol used by doctors in The Netherlands to identify situations in which euthanasia might be appropriate. Their views appear in a special issue of the *Journal of Medical Ethics*.

The Groningen Protocol was introduced in 2005 in The Netherlands. Its development was triggered by the case of a baby girl with excruciatingly painful and progressive skin disease whose parents asked doctors to end her suffering. The request was refused on the grounds that the doctors concerned could be prosecuted for murder. The young patient died three months later.

But protocol author, Dr Eduard Verhagen, says that evidence from two national surveys of end of life care in 1995 and 2001 indicates that doctors were making decisions to end a child's life for humanitarian reasons before 2005, but were not being open about it.

Practice Already Existed

In 1% of deaths among children under the age of 12 months during this period, drugs were given with the explicit intention of hastening death, leading the author to conclude that between 15 and 20 children every year had their lives ended in this way in The Netherlands. Yet only three such cases were officially reported.

The protocol stipulates that five criteria must be met before euthanasia can even be considered: diagnosis and prognosis beyond doubt; presence of hopeless and unbearable suffering; a second independent medical opinion to confirm the first; the consent of both parents; and compliance with strict medical standards.

But the protocol's publication provoked a storm of controversy, with critics suggesting it would open the floodgates for euthanasia of newborns.

So the author reviewed all reported cases of infant euthanasia between 2001 and 2010.

In 95% of cases, treatment was withheld or withdrawn. In 60% of cases this was because the child had an incurable condition from which they were soon going to die. In the remainder, it was the child's quality of life that prompted the decision.

Some parents may prefer the option of euthanasia for very sick babies to termination of pregnancy, because the level of certainty around diagnosis and prognosis is much clearer after birth.

But in the five years following the introduction of the protocol, the proportion of euthanasia cases dropped to two—both babies with lethal epidermolysis bullosa, a condition that causes extensive internal and external blistering of the skin.

Increased Certainty

The author says that the introduction of screening and a subsequent rise in terminations for inborn abnormalities after 2007 might help explain these figures. Or it might be that there is still no consensus among doctors on what constitutes euthanasia—a situation that might be clarified when the Dutch Medical Association publishes its report on the issue, later this year [2013].

But he suggests that some parents may prefer the option of euthanasia for very sick babies to termination of pregnancy, because the level of certainty around diagnosis and prognosis is much clearer after birth, and they can discuss all the treatment options available, including palliative care.

"If all the stakeholders conclude that the prognosis is very grim, the baby's condition is judged as one with sustained and intolerable suffering, and the parents request euthanasia, why should that not be permissible as an alternative to second trimester termination?", argues Dr Verhagen.

And he questions what the moral difference is between withholding food/water and treatment and euthanasia.

"I'd like to argue that for some patients and/or parents, neonatal euthanasia might be preferable . . . especially in situations where every hour, every day of life imposes an intolerable burden on the baby and the parents," he concludes.

Hastening Death

In an accompanying editorial, Professor Julian Savulescu, points out that withholding treatment with the intention of hastening death is "not uncommon" in neonatal intensive care.

"The active withdrawal of life-prolonging medical care (an intentional act that kills, even if not necessarily with the intention to kill) is a standard part of medical practice in relation to people who experience severe disability and suffering, including newborns," he writes.

"Discussions of infanticide [allowing the newborn to die] should be contextualised in those practices that end life, which society already accepts, even if they are euphemistically redescribed," he writes.

"Infanticide is an important issue and worthy of scholarly attention because it touches on an area of concern that few societies have had the courage to tackle openly and honestly: euthanasia," he adds.

Organizations to Contact

The editors have compiled the following list of organizations concerned with the issues debated in this book. The descriptions are derived from materials provided by the organizations themselves. All have publications or information available for interested readers. The list was compiled on the date of publication of the present volume; names, addresses, phone and fax numbers, and e-mail and Internet addresses may change. Be aware that many organizations take several weeks or longer to respond to inquiries, so allow as much time as possible.

American Foundation for Suicide Prevention (AFSP)
120 Wall St., 29th Floor, New York, NY   10005
(212) 363-3500 • fax: (212) 363-6237
e-mail: inquiry@afsp.org
website: www.afsp.org

Formerly known as the American Suicide Foundation, the American Foundation for Suicide Prevention (AFSP) supports scientific research on depression and suicide, educates the public and professionals on the recognition and treatment of depressed and suicidal individuals, and provides support programs for those coping with the loss of a loved one to suicide. It opposes the legalization of physician-assisted suicide. The AFSP publishes educational and self-help pamphlets as well as policy statements on key issues that have an impact on suicide prevention.

American Life League (ALL)
PO Box 1350, Stafford, VA   22555
(703) 659-4171 • fax: (703) 659-2586
e-mail: info@all.org
website: www.all.org

The American Life League (ALL) is a pro-life organization that provides information and educational materials to organizations opposed to physician-assisted suicide and abortion. Its publications include pamphlets, reports, and weekly newsletters, all of which may be downloaded directly from its website.

American Medical Association (AMA)

515 N. State St., Chicago, IL   60654
(800) 621-8335
website: www.ama-assn.org

Founded in 1847, the American Medical Association (AMA) is the primary professional association of physicians in the United States. It disseminates information concerning medical breakthroughs, medical and health legislation, educational standards for physicians, and other issues concerning medicine and health care. It opposes physician-assisted suicide. The AMA operates a library and offers many publications, including its weekly journal, *JAMA*, the weekly newspaper *American Medical News*, and journals covering specific types of medical specialties.

American Society of Law, Medicine, and Ethics (ASLME)

765 Commonwealth Ave., Suite 1634, Boston, MA   02215
(617) 262-4990 • fax: (617) 437-7596
e-mail: info@aslme.org
website: www.aslme.org

The American Society of Law, Medicine, and Ethics (ASLME) is a membership organization consisting of physicians, attorneys, health-care administrators, and others interested in the relationship between law, medicine and ethics. The organization publishes the quarterlies *American Journal of Law & Medicine* and *Journal of Law, Medicine & Ethics* and books such as *Legal and Ethical Aspects of Treating Critically and Terminally Ill Patients*. Its website hosts blogs, forums, and other interactive resources.

Compassion & Choices

PO Box 101810, Denver, CO   80250
(800) 247-7421 • fax: (866) 312-2690

e-mail: info@compassionandchoices.org
website: www.compassionandchoices.org

Formerly known as the Hemlock Society, Compassion & Choices is the country's largest death with dignity advocacy group. The nonprofit works to improve patients' rights and choices at the end of life, and it assists clients with advance directives, local service referrals, and pain and symptom management. The organization asserts constitutional protection for aid-in-dying and its team of litigators and legislative experts work on shaping polices for end of life care, including advance directives for patients and mandates for physicians to receive pain and palliative care training. The group maintains an extensive web archive of articles, literature, and videos.

Death with Dignity National Center (DDNC)

520 SW 6th Ave., Suite 1220, Portland, OR 97204
(503) 228-4415 • fax: (503) 967-7064
e-mail: info@deathwithdignity.org
website: www.deathwithdignity.org

The goal of the Death with Dignity National Center (DDNC) is to provide information, education, research, and support for the preservation, implementation, and promotion of death with dignity laws which allow a terminally ill, mentally competent adult the right to request and receive a prescription to hasten death under certain specific safeguards. The DDNC welcomes student inquiries and has educational materials available through its website, including an archive of their newsletter, *The Dignity Report.*

Dying with Dignity

55 Eglinton Ave. East, Suite 802, Toronto, Ontario M4P 1G8
  Canada
(800) 495-6156 • fax: (416) 486-5562
e-mail: info@dyingwithdignity.ca
website: www.dyingwithdignity.ca

Dying with Dignity is a national nonprofit organization working to improve quality of dying and to expand end of life choices in Canada. The group advocates for improved hospice and palliative care services as well as legislative change that would increase end of life care options, including physician aid-in-dying. The organization maintains an informative blog and extensive library of information concerning end of life issues, death with dignity, and care resources.

Euthanasia Research and Guidance Organization (ERGO)
24829 Norris Lane, Junction City, OR   97448-9559
(541) 998-1873
e-mail: ergo@efn.org
website: www.finalexit.org

The Euthanasia Research and Guidance Organization (ERGO) advocates for the passage of laws permitting physician-assisted suicide for the advanced terminally ill and the irreversibly ill who are suffering unbearably. It seeks to accomplish its goals by providing research data, addressing the public through the media, and helping raise campaign funds. The organization's website contains extensive materials, including essays, frequently asked questions, a glossary of terms, and other resources.

Final Exit Network
PO Box 10071, Tallahassee, FL   32302
(866) 654-9156
e-mail: PR@finalexitnetwork.org
website: www.finalexitnetwork.org

The Final Exit Network is a volunteer-operated nonprofit that fights for the right of competent adults to choose to end their lives when they suffer from irreversible physical illness, intractable pain, or a constellation of chronic, progressive physical disabilities. The organization promotes the use of advance directives and other legal means to document an individual's final wishes, and it sponsors research into new peaceful and reliable methods to end life. The group offers free services to all who qualify, including information, home visits if possible, and a compassionate presence for individual and family. The Final Exit website offers information about the group's philosophy and services, as well as extensive learning resources, research, and news updates.

The Hastings Center

21 Malcolm Gordon Rd., Garrison, NY 10524-4125
(845) 424-4040 • fax: (845) 424-4545
e-mail: mail@thehastingscenter.org
website: www.thehastingscenter.org

The Hastings Center is a nonpartisan research institution dedicated to bioethics and the public interest. Since 1969, the Center has played a key role in raising ethical questions in response to advances in medicine, biological sciences, and social sciences. It does not take a position on issues such as euthanasia and assisted suicide but offers a forum for exploration and debate. The Center publishes numerous books, papers, guidelines, and journals, including the *Hastings Center Report*, and its website includes many resources relevant to this topic, including the reports "A Suicide Right for the Mentally Ill? A Swiss Case Opens a New Debate," "Dying with Dignity," and "Euthanasia in Belgium: The Untold Story."

Human Life International

4 Family Life Lane, Front Royal, VA 22630
(800) 549-LIFE • fax: (540) 622-6247
e-mail: hli@hli.org
website: www.hli.org

Human Life International is a pro-life research, educational, and service organization. It opposes euthanasia and assisted suicide. The group publishes books such as *Death Without Dignity* as well as other materials. The organization's website provides extensive resources, including in-house publications such as *HLI Commentaries, Spirit and Life Archive* and *Mission Reports Archive.*

National Hospice and Palliative Care Organization (NHPCO)

1731 King St., Suite 100, Alexandria, VA   22314
(703) 837-1500 • fax: (703) 837-1233
e-mail: nhpco_info@nhpco.org
website: www.nhpco.org

The National Hospice and Palliative Care Organization (NHPCO) is committed to improving end of life care and expanding access to hospice care with the goal of profoundly enhancing the quality of life for people dying in America. The organization opposes euthanasia and assisted suicide. In addition to its main website, the organization operates a related educational site, Caring Connections (www.caringinfo.org), which offers extensive resources in keeping with NHPCO's mission and philosophy.

Patient Choices at End of Life—Vermont

708 Wake Robin Dr., Shelburne, VT   05482
(802) 985-9473
e-mail: info@patientchoices.org
website: www.patientchoices.org

Patient Choices is an advocacy organization that seeks to educate Vermonters about end of life options and to influence policy, regulations, and practice that affect the terminally ill. It works to promote the best possible pain control and palliative and hospice care, and to enable terminally ill patients to choose the timing and manner of dying if even the best of care fails to prevent or alleviate unbearable suffering. The organization's website provides information about their work in Vermont as well as links to more general articles and resources that deal with end of life care and assisted-death advocacy.

Patients Rights Council

PO Box 760, Steubenville, OH   43952
(800) 958-5678
website: www.patientsrightscouncil.org

Formerly known as the International Task Force on Euthanasia and Assisted-Suicide, the Patients Rights Council works to ensure that a patient's right to receive care and compassion is not replaced by a doctor's right to prescribe poison or administer a lethal injection. The organization opposes euthanasia, assisted suicide, and policies that threaten the lives of the medically vulnerable. The group pursues its mission through networking, publishing materials, maintaining the Frank Reed Memorial Library, and working with lawyers in the field of bioethics. The group's newsletter, *The ITF Update*, is archived online, and its website features a variety of news updates and information about pain control, advance directives, and end of life legal issues.

Bibliography

Books

Arthur Caplan, James McCartney, and Dominic Sisti, eds. *The Case of Terri Schiavo: Ethics at the End of Life*. New York: Prometheus, 2006.

Roland Chia *The Right to Die? A Christian Response to Euthanasia*. Singapore: Armour Publishing, 2009.

William Colby *Long Goodbye: The Deaths of Nancy Cruzan*, 5th ed. Carlsbad, CA: Hay House, 2003.

William Colby *Unplugged: Reclaiming Our Right to Die in America*. New York: AMACOM, 2007.

Richard N. Côté *In Search of Gentle Death: The Fight for Your Right to Die with Dignity*. Mt. Pleasant, SC: Corinthian Books, 2012.

Jon Eisenberg *The Right vs. the Right to Die: Lessons from the Terri Schiavo Case and How to Stop It from Happening Again*. New York: Harper One, 2006.

Doris Fleischer and Frieda Zames *The Disability Rights Movement: From Charity to Confrontation*. Philadelphia: Temple University Press, 2011.

Erik Leipoldt · *Euthanasia and Disability Perspective.* Saarbrücken, Germany: VDM Verlag Dr. Müller, 2010.

John Mitchel · *Understanding Assisted Suicide: Nine Issues to Consider.* Ann Arbor: University of Michigan Press, 2007.

Neal Nicol, Harry Wylie, and Jack Kevorkian · *Between the Dying and the Dead: Dr. Jack Kevorkian's Life and the Battle to Legalize Euthanasia.* Madison: University of Wisconsin Press, 2006.

Robert Orfal · *Death with Dignity: The Case for Legalizing Physician-Assisted Dying and Euthanasia.* Minneapolis: Mill City Press, 2011.

Timothy Quill and Margaret P. Battin, eds. · *Physician-Assisted Dying: The Case for Palliative Care and Patient Choice.* Baltimore: Johns Hopkins University Press, 2004.

Michael Schiavo and Michael Hirsh · *Terri: The Truth.* Hialeah, FL: Dutton Adult, 2006.

Sidney Wanzer and Joseph Glenmullen · *To Die Well: Your Right to Comfort, Calm, and Choice in the Last Days of Life.* Cambridge, MA: Da Capo Press, 2008.

Periodicals and Internet Sources

JoNel Aleccia · "One Man's Journey," NBC News, April 10, 2012. www.nbcnews.com.

Charlotte Allen · "Back off! I'm Not Dead Yet," *Washington Post*, October 14, 2007.

George Annas — "Congress, Controlled Substances, and Physician-Assisted Suicide—Elephants in Mouseholes," *The New England Journal of Medicine*, vol. 354, no. 10, March 9, 2006.

Jacob Appel — "Mercy Killing: When Love & Law Conflict," *Huffington Post*, September 25, 2009. www.huffingtonpost.com.

Brook Barnes — "Unflinching End-of-Life Moments," *New York Times*, January 24, 2011.

BBC — "Tony Nicklinson's Legal Fight for Right to Die," BBC.com, August 22, 2012.

Daniel Bergner — "Death in the Family," *New York Times*, December 2, 2007.

Jane Brody — "A Heartfelt Appeal for a Graceful Exit," *New York Times*, February 5, 2008.

Robbie Brown — "Arrests Draw New Attention to Assisted Suicide," *New York Times*, March 10, 2009.

Daniel Callahan — "Organized Obfuscation: Advocacy for Physician-Assisted Suicide," *Hastings Center Report*, vol. 38, no. 5, September/October 2008.

Art Caplan — "Ethicist: Mass. Should Legalize Physician-Assisted Suicide," NBC News, November 1, 2012. www.nbcnews.com.

CNN

"The Case in Support of Euthanasia,"
August 16, 2012. www.cnn.com.

Diane Coleman
and Stephen
Drake

"Disability Discrimination," Hastings
Center Bioethics Forum, July 11,
2012. www.thehastingscenter.org
/bioethicsforum.

Ezekiel
Emanuelmar

"Whose Right to Die," *The Altantic*,
March 1, 1997.

Fiona Godlee

"Assisted Dying," *British Medical
Journal*, vol. 344, June 14, 2012.

Chris Hampson

"In Controversial Move, BBC Airs
Assisted Suicide on TV," NBC News,
June 14, 2011. www.nbcnews.com.

Nat Hentoff

"Terri Schiavo: Judicial Murder,"
Village Voice, March 22, 2005.

Michael Kirkland

"The Right to Die vs. the Value of
Life," UPI, March 21, 2010.
www.upi.com.

Mike Latona

"Who Decides the Right to Die?"
Catholic Courier, February 2, 2010.

Barbara
Coombs Lee

"End-of-Life Bill Empowers Sick
Patients," *Los Angeles Times*, October
29, 2008.

Barbara
Coombs Lee

"Life, Liberty and the Right to Die,"
USA Today, April 2, 2013.

Shawn Levy

"'How to Die in Oregon' Takes Top
Documentary Prize at Sundance,"
The Oregonian, January 29, 2011.

Tamar Lewin — "Nancy Cruzan Dies, Outlived by a Debate Over the Right to Die," *New York Times*, December 27, 1990.

Justin Lowe — "HBO Documentary Probes Oregon's Euthanasia Law," Reuters, January 29, 2011. www.reuters.com.

Diana Lynn — "Life and Death Tug of War—The Whole Terri Schiavo Story," WorldNetDaily, March 24, 2005. www.wnd.com.

MSNBC — "Terri Schiavo Dies, but Battle Continues," March 31, 2005. www.nbcnews.com.

Tony Nicklinson — "Assisted Dying Debate: Tony Nicklinson in His Own Words," BBC, June 19, 2012. www.bbcnews.com.

Brian O'Neel — "Still Troubled by Terri Schiavo's Death, but Inspired, Too," *National Catholic Register*, January 10, 2013.

Stanton Price — "Different Assisted-Suicide Groups, One Goal," *Los Angeles Times*, March 27, 2009.

Timothy Quill — "Physician-Assisted Death in the United States: Are the Existing 'Last Resorts' Enough?" *Hastings Center Report*, vol. 38, no. 5, September/October 2008.

Timothy Quill and Diane Meier — "The Big Chill: Inserting the DEA Into End-of-Life Care," *New England Journal of Medicine*, vol. 354, no. 1, January 5, 2006.

Ragged Edge "Why Disability Rights Activists Oppose Physician Assisted Suicide," January 18, 2006. www.ragged edgemagazine.com.

Reuters "Paralyzed British Men Fight Right-to-Die Case in Court," Fox News, May 13, 2013. www.foxnews.com.

Darshak Sanghavi "Helping My Father Die," *Boston Globe*, July 3, 2007.

Mallory Simon "'Harrowing,' or 'Disgraceful?' Assisted Suicide Documentary Sparks Debate," CNN, June 15, 2011. www.cnn.com.

James Thunder "Helen Keller, Anne Sullivan, and Assisted Suicide," *The American Spectator*, January 17, 2013.

Susan Tolle et al. "Characteristics and Proportion of Dying Oregonians Who Personally Consider Physician-Assisted Suicide," *Journal of Clinical Ethics*, Summer 2004.

Agnes van der Heide et al. "End-of-Life Practices in The Netherlands Under the Euthanasia Act," *New England Journal of Medicine*, May 10, 2007.

Michael Wenham "Choosing to Die Misses the Depth of Life," *The Guardian*, June 15, 2011.

Gregor Wolbring   "Why Disability Rights Movements
Do Not Support Euthanasia:
Safeguards Broken Beyond Repair,"
independentliving.org, 1998.

Mackenzie Yang   "Paralyzed British Man Fights for the
Right to Die," *Time*, April 22, 2013.

Index

CPSIA information can be obtained
at www.ICGtesting.com
Printed in the USA
FFOW02n0242250914
7599FF